THE NATURE
OF CRICKET

Graham Coster is the publisher of Safe Haven Books. His other books include *Snow Stopped Play: The Mysterious World of the Cricket Ground in Winter* and *The Flying Boat That Fell to Earth*. He writes a cricket blog called Hammock Innings.

THE NATURE OF CRICKET

OF CRICKET

A NATURAL HISTORY OF
THE CRICKET GROUND

Graham Coster

SAFE HAVEN

First published 2021 by Safe Haven Books Ltd
12 Chinnocks Wharf
14 Narrow Street
London E14 8DJ
www.safehavenbooks.co.uk

A catalogue record for this book is available from the British Library.

ISBN 978 1 8384051 1 3

10 9 8 7 6 5 4 3 2 1

The Safe Haven team on *The Nature of Cricket*:
Graham Coster, Ashley Western, David Welch

Designed by Ashley Western in Filosofia and Brandon

Printed and bound in the EU by Elcograf S. p. A.

FSC
www.fsc.org
MIX
Paper from
responsible sources
FSC® C115118

Frontispiece: ↑ County cricket at leafy Colwyn Bay.
↓ Pigeons outnumber players at the Oval.

For Mathew Frith:
peerless naturalist, oldest friend

CONTENTS

AUTHOR'S NOTE

I'm aware that any serious work of natural history like a New Naturalist would include the Latin names of every species. But for me, and this book, a cuckoo is a cuckoo and a hare is a hare, and I'm afraid most of the time gulls are just seagulls.

INTRODUCTION

t was an auspicious start to an Ashes summer. 2015: when the five-match series in England would go down to the final Test for England to secure a 3–2 victory at the Oval. In the lead-up to the first I was down at Canterbury at the end of June for the preliminary tour match against Kent. A packed St Lawrence Ground for the Saturday, a radiantly sunny day, and now the young Kent fast bowler Matt Hunn had dismissed Mitchell Marsh to take five Australian wickets. 'Old-fashioned cricket', murmured Simon Wilde, the *Sunday Times*'s cricket correspondent, approvingly when we bumped into each other during the luncheon interval.

But something else helped make it a red-letter day. There may have been Mitchell Johnson walking out to bat, Ryan Harris fielding in the deep just in front of me, Brad Haddin signing autographs in the club shop . . . but suddenly, as Matt Hunn was loping in again from the pavilion end, I found myself swivelling my binoculars away from the action and up, up – yes! The slender wings, that boomerang-ish outline, like a large swift, skimming about the sky: *Falco subbuteo*: the small, graceful, summer-visiting falcon, snapping insects out of the air, the underparts – could I just make out? – a characteristic rufous-red . . .

A hobby! Had a wicket fallen it would still have been important to keep the bins trained to make sure.

It was a rare enough sighting to have stayed part of that day, as

has the red kite sailing above over Uxbridge cricket ground that enlivened a rather slow day's play on a flat wicket between Middlesex and Warwickshire, and the stiffly civil difference of opinion out in the middle at the County Ground in Taunton during another lunch interval a few years ago when a fellow spectator was unwise enough helpfully to point out to my friend Stephen a far-flung

Sussex County Cricket Ground. Hove.

peregrine across the River Tone. Stephen is the nature writer Stephen Moss: he will cheerfully admit his comparative ignorance about cricket, but he does know his birds, and has led expeditions around the globe to find them. 'I don't think so,' said Stephen firmly, his powerful Swarovskis fixed on the distant speck. 'I think you'll find that's a sparrowhawk.'

But at least we were all looking.

This is not a book about a birdwatcher who is interested in cricket (though birds do come into it, including some pretty rare ones). It's about the natural life of a cricket ground – all of it.

We cannot but start with the ground. *The. Ground.* Earth. The bare

← A hobby (note rufous underparts).
↑ The County Ground, Hove, c. 1900: still an expanse of grass.

soil of the land. You can't start with anything else. And whereas other sports set about constructing their pitches, their courts, their tracks, their stadia, by covering up that earth as quickly as possible and piling towers and cantilevers of concrete and masonry and girdering and cabling on top, cricket – at least until recently, and still never entirely, does not.

On the earth you level a field – or maybe there was one there already. A cricket field is what cricket is played on. Sometimes it is even shared, during the close season, with the odd sheep or pony. Usually – ideally – it is surrounded with trees: to demarcate the prop-erty, to break the wind, to protect the houses beyond from six hits, to

Abinger Hammer in the Surrey Hills.

create a natural arena. It might even be next to the sea.

And if you create — or simply leave as it was — a natural arena, then the rest of the natural world stays too: the birds, the animals, the flowers, the mosses, the lichens. Test matches have been lost to fungi (see Chapter 4). From the point of view of a hobby everything on earth is habitat: a potential place to live, or to hunt; there is just good habitat and bad habitat. A cricket field, girded with trees, the silence broken only by the sporadic smack of a drive, a ragged appeal or the soft applause rattling like aspen leaves, is fine hunting habitat on a summer afternoon when the air is thick with flies. The Canterbury ring road a mile or two into town is not.

So there's a reason why I saw that hobby at the St Lawrence Ground (as I still call it). Situated out along the Dover Road amid prosperous, leafy streets on the southern edge of Canterbury, it is indeed an old-fashioned, or at least traditional, cricket ground. It will not be hosting The Hundred. Bounded by trees at its southern Nackington Road End, and still with a bank of greensward beyond the boundary running up to another belt of trees along its eastern perimeter, broad enough for picnics and promenades, it is still expansive and low-rise enough to retain the feel of a field.

Or it was back in 2015.

Even then it was not what it had been, by a long way. My first visit had been back in the late eighties: a County Championship match in 1988 against Somerset, with the great Australian Steve Waugh playing a season for the visitors, and smiting quite the finest innings I have ever sat at a cricket ground to see: a chanceless 161 – not a single stroke not played along the ground, in the almost lost art of getting to the pitch of the ball and playing down the line; subsequently I saw the West Indian and Pakistani tourists, and Graham Gooch wading out to the middle with his characteristic gait as though in Wellingtons, to hit a typically inevitable century for Essex. In those days (he says, old enough now to be able to), I recall you entered the ground up a lovely avenue of trees – I wish I had taken note then of what they were. Limes, I like to think. If you had a car, you turned right off the driveway just inside the gates and parked it in a large field. Behind the pavilion were tennis courts.

That all went around the turn of the century. The avenue of trees disappeared, and a Sainsbury's convenience store was plonked down at the entrance. The car park was covered with houses. So were the tennis courts. But at least the Dover Road side of the ground remained an open sweep of grassy bank to match the one opposite, and the ground's unique, historic feature, the Kent lime – a solitary lime tree – stood actually inside the boundary.

But since that hobby day at the Australians there has been more change, and now, down that western side of the ground, stretches a rampart of retirement flats: not just up to where the boundary was, it seems, but over it, and the Kent lime is now on the wrong (in St Lawrence

Ground terms) side of the boundary. I only know this from pictures: I haven't been back since. I don't know if you can still see a hobby there in summer, but that field certainly seems smaller than I remember it, and more grass has been covered with bricks and concrete.

You can overdo the cricket nostalgia. I don't imagine Elgar or 'Lark Ascending' on the soundtrack when I think of cricket matches past. A lot of county cricket grounds used to be dumps. At least one still is a bit. The attitude towards non-members at certain county grounds in the Home Counties can be unwelcoming to the point of segregationist.

The St Lawrence Ground, Canterbury: the top-left-hand corner and entire right-hand side have since been built on.

Ultimately you do play a game of cricket to win (although, to a spectator of what we now have to call 'the red-ball game', it is one of the few games that affords the pleasure of just watching a whole day's 'play'). But, as my friend Mathew Frith, Head of Conservation at the London Wildlife Trust, reflected, 'It must be one of the few sports which is played more or less at the pace of nature?' Exactly – if you play it right. (Some would say it's about as exciting as watching the grass grow.) Cricket is seasonal: it starts with the end of spring and it ends with the start of autumn. It follows the waxing and waning light of a whole day. Sometimes a passage of play does creep along at *snail's pace*.

In no other sport is distraction such an intrinsic part of the spectating experience: during a day's cricket there is time for the mind and the attention to wander from the contest out in the middle: time to *notice* things – everything! – from the passing pigeons ritually itemised

In 1997 England played at idyllic Fitzherbert Park in New Zealand.

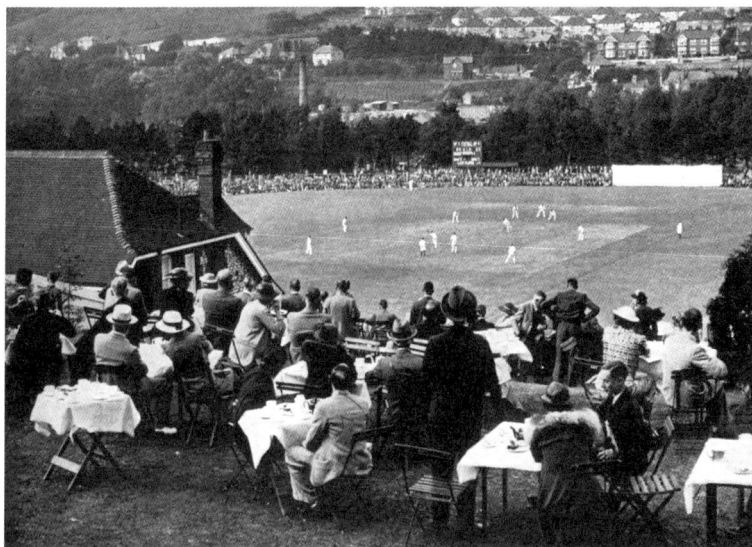

by Henry Blofeld during his *Test Match Special* commentaries to the urban foxes, given free run of the Oval outfield by the Covid lockdown, that increasingly fascinated Tuffers while he commentated remotely from the press box on the 2021 Test series out in Sri Lanka. Watching a proper cricket match is the most mindful experience to be had.

The great Neville Cardus is usually apotheosised for his celebrations of a cricketer's 'knightly sword' or 'winged batsmanship' (Victor Trumper, both times). But what I like even more about Cardus is how he made a point of writing about the *occasion*: the venue; the weather; the atmosphere. He was never just interested in who won. 'The Kent innings began at noon under a dome of glass all stained blue,' he wrote in his magnificent account of Kent against Lancashire at Dover in 1926, amid 'the June charm and flavours of a field all gay with tents and waving colours'. If he had seen a hobby up in that dome of glass

---

'A field all gay with tents and waving colours': Neville Cardus's beloved Crabble ground in Dover, 1938.

he'd have told you. It would have been just as important as the cricket. It was still about the game.

And what I mourn most about the virtual eradication of daily match reports of the County Championship from the sports pages of the newspapers are those accounts in similar vein from proper cricket writers who noticed everything. Matthew Engel used to. I have no recollection of even the teams involved, but I'm pretty sure I recall Mike Selvey writing in the *Guardian* one morning of how the players had turned up first thing – was it at Grace Road in Leicester? – to find a hedgehog had managed to climb up and entangle itself in one of the nets. Today's IPL-bound professionals and county chief executives preoccupied with paddle scoops and conferencing facilities will roll their eyes, but that, as much as anything, was what I used to read the cricket reports for.

You can't separate cricket from the natural world. The batsman[1] wields an implement crafted from the finest British-grown willow wood. More grass left on the wicket means help for the bowlers. A lush outfield means hard work for the batsmen trying to hit a boundary. Some squares – Northampton, Southampton – are laid on soil that seems to keep them irremediably flat, or true, whatever is done to them. Others – Taunton, or Cyderabad – are more friable, and so are the innings played out on them. The groundsman's job is a daily battle with the elements: rain, heat, damp, weeds, pigeons. The weather, in all its minutely fluctuating nuances, even down to the air pressure, is such an active protagonist that an entire book has been written just about the interaction of the game with rain.[2] But I'd go further and say that when steps are taken to separate cricket from its natural history

---

[1] Sadly 'batswoman', with its superheroine connotations, does not yet seem to have achieved currency.

[2] Andrew Hignell, *Rain Stops Play* (2002). Readers reasonably expecting consideration of the weather as an essential component of the natural history of the cricket ground are referred to this title and the author's own *Snow Stopped Play* (2015).

– by turning a cricket ground into a stadium; by subjecting a cricket ground to death by a thousand cuts until it risks surviving just as a kind of lawn-feature amid a sea of development, which is what increasingly seems to be happening; by focusing just on the dismissals, the 'maximums', who won – it loses some of its . . . nature.

No-one interested in the natural world and involved with book publishing can be unaware of the greatest venture to link both: the Collins New Naturalist series. Founded in 1945, it has now reached, at the time of writing, its 144th title. These monographs are unashamedly completist, scholarly, academic works, disserting variously on Gulls, Slugs and Snails or Ants, on whole regions like Pembrokeshire, or on topics like Farming and Birds or Vegetation of Britain and Ireland.

The Parks, Oxford: a natural place to watch cricket.

Once I'd come to cherish the indivisibility of cricket and the natural world I'd idly wish someone would come up with a New Naturalist called *Cricket Grounds* (at least partly for the pleasure of seeing what Robert Gillmor, the artist whose magnificent linocuts decorate the series' jackets, would have come up with for the cover).

Such a volume, however, would, in the New Naturalist way, have had to be about 600 pages long and retail at £60, and even I probably wouldn't have read it all the way through. I definitely couldn't have been bothered to write it. But still – what *would* have been in it? Since my publishing philosophy has always been to publish the books I wanted to read but that didn't exist, I thought I'd have a go at my own alternative to a volume that will almost certainly never be written. 'That sounds *barkingly* eccentric,' pronounced a friend I ran the idea by, which was just the encouragement I needed. *Tour d'horizon* rather than completist, this is a lot shorter, and cheaper, but still a new naturalist: the cricket naturalist.

Graham Coster
May 2021

01

GRASS

You don't of course, *have* to play cricket on grass. You can play it on the beach, though this is a pastime more akin to frisbee-throwing for which a tiny plastic bat is *de rigueur*. You can stage games on ice, as was frequently attempted in the nineteenth century when ponds and lakes routinely froze over in a hard winter. Sheffield Park in Sussex was one such venue, the Marquis of Abergavenny's Eridge Castle another. The stunt has since become an annual tradition at St Moritz, and was repeated in 1985 down in the Antarctic by two teams of international scientists and environmentalists 700 kilometres from the South Pole, in arguably the southernmost cricket match ever played, on a pitch rolled by Hercules transport plane.

And you can get away with playing it, without novelty value, on a surface entirely devoid of grass. Alfred Shaw's England XI that toured Australia in 1884/5 broke their voyage in Suez to play against the Army, Navy and Residents on 'a plain of sand', while *Wisden* reported in 1995 that cricket was planned to return to its traditional ground on Ascension Island, beside the church (located inside the boundary) on the former army parade ground, which consisted of 'rolled volcanic ash, with not a blade of grass in sight', necessitating the use of composite balls as 'a leather ball would be torn to shreds'.

But grass is the default option. What kind of grass, though, and what do you do with your field?

While traditionally 'fine fescues and bentgrasses were used for cricket wickets due to their inherent tolerance for close mowing' (I am of course googling this),[1] nowadays it's 'a mixture of perennial ryegrass'. For the outfield: creeping red fescues, turf-type turf-type perennial ryegrasses, smooth-stalked meadow grasses and bents. All this means little (correction: nothing) to me, but the grass on the wicket obviously has to be hardy enough to withstand a regular shaving within a millimetre of its life down to billiard-table smoothness

1 Germinalamenity.com, a grass seed supplier.

without simply dying, whereas you want new grass on the playing surface to grow quickly and lushly to produce a 'uniform, wear-tolerant sward'.

But that's if you start from scratch. Most village cricket fields started out as a field. Here is Edmund Blunden, back in the Edwardian era, nostalgic about a childhood cricket ground in East Anglia,

> with perhaps a stripling stream flowing between the area
> of the wickets and the hills and holes of the outfield, or a
> couple of willows just behind square leg. I still remember
> with incurable discontent the spoiling of my rare big hit by
> an intervening oak or a sweet cow who looked round from
> her study of grasses with mild surprise as the ball slapped
> her rich coat.

Back in the mid-nineteenth century even Lord's was still grazed by sheep, as an 1837 watercolour by W. H. Prior shows. The entomologist and village cricketer Tim Gardiner, who plays for the Chignal

Lord's in 1837: still a field grazed by sheep in W. H. Prior's watercolour.

club in south Essex, writes in his excellent paper 'More runs, fewer crickets', published in the *Bulletin of the Amateur Entomologist's Society*, of cricket being played 'in a meadow which during the week was used for grazing the local cows' as late as the pre-war era. The local grounds in the 1930s and 1940s

> were in essence local meadows, which were cut annually (at best) with a scythe, or grazed by cows or horses. The resulting outfields were often covered in tall grass all over (some players mention grass as high as a foot!) and the actual pitches (or wickets) were said to be treacherous; both factors combined made batting difficult, as the batsman could never rely on how high the ball was going to bounce off the pitch (e.g. it either bounced around the batsman's ankles or his nose!). If the unlucky batsman did manage to hit the ball, the long grass in the outfield slowed the progress of it towards the boundary and made it difficult to get more than one run.

In that 'bygone age' 50 would often be a winning total, and teams could be bowled out for less than 10.

But after the war, as Tim explains, gang mowers began to be used to cut outfields, which 'has led to much more intensive management

← Chignal Cricket Club in Essex.
→ Untended grass outside the pavilion at the abandoned Pleshey ground, Essex.

. . . with it possible to cut the entire playing area to an extremely low sward height on a weekly basis' – shorter than 2 cm – which may make the ball travel more quickly and have enabled a rustic batsman at last to hit a 4, but has also 'led to the eradication of weeds and tall grassland to such an extent that outfields now resemble intensively grazed pasture or amenity "parkland"'. The consequences for biodiversity – the flowers, plants and insects that used to live in a hay meadow – are, as we shall see in future chapters, considerable.

Nature gets a further bashing at the cricket grounds of the present, of course. Here is how much fertiliser is recommended annually nowadays per hectare for an average cricket square:

Nitrogen: 80-120 kg
Phosphorus: 20-49 kg
Potassium: 40-100 kg

Kilogrammes! Makes the ground look like the Augusta National, but it all runs off into the water table.

Then there's the problem that, the more you turn a cricket ground into a stadium, the more the ever-higher-towering stands block out the natural light. The new Wembley Stadium was the notorious trailblazer: so insufficient was the light getting onto the playing surface when this vast concrete bowl opened that in the first four years the pitch had to be completely re-laid no fewer than ten times. 'It's a disgrace,' spluttered Harry Redknapp after his Spurs side had lost to Portsmouth in the 2010 FA Cup semi-final. 'You have to spend the whole time making sure you don't fall over. That can't be right, can it? How can you play on a pitch you can't stand up on?'

Football clubs now resort to various dubious measures (from the point of view of the natural world) to prevent this kind of thing. One is to drench the grass with the simulated sunlight from huge light frames moved across the pitch – the equivalent of your lawn going for a sunbed. The other is to weave a playing surface out of a combination of grass grass and plastic grass. Most new stadiums go down this route. I see this mutant love-child is 'recently available for cricket and golf'. If I were king for a day and could pass just one law I would ban plastic grass.

A number of rugby clubs, league and union, have already gone the whole hog and installed 100% plastic pitches. The cost savings, of course, on groundstaff, mowers, fertilisers, watering, not to mention lost revenue from games cancelled owing to waterlogging or bottomless mud, are substantial, but this is still – 3G, the official terminology, sounds far too techno – just *plastic* grass. So far cricket has not gone down this route, or even talked about it.

But, you see, with the advent of the Hundred, there is *another way* ... When what used to be the game of cricket is reduced to the single party trick of six-hitting, you don't need an outfield like a billiard table. No-one's going to be essaying a cover drive. So why not make the Hundred the game not just of a hundred balls but of *a hundred species* – the most biodiverse form of the game of all? Let the outfield grow into a magnificent wild-flower meadow buzzing with invertebrates, dancing with butterflies – we can re-wild the Rose Bowl! The ECB: the Ecological Cricket Board! What does it matter if the fielding side are standing knee-deep in horseshoe vetch as they watch the latest maximum sail overhead?

I am surprised no-one has suggested this.

But as the county cricket clubs seek to re-develop their headquarters into stadia, the consequence is an inexorable loss of greensward. When I look at some other sports this seems – in marketing terms, never mind ecological – all the more baffling. What would be the two most consistently successful annual sporting events, whether you think of the demand for tickets, the prestige of winning, the goldmine of broadcasting rights, or the simple visual spectacle you see every year on TV? I'd say: the Masters, and Wimbledon. And the key to both

is: *they don't change it.* Perhaps Wimbledon could save a fortune by going over to synthetic courts; the Augusta National could build five-star hotels and condos right up to the fairways. But the value of those events is in their enduring, unchanging, natural beauty: the ivy-clad walls of the Centre Court, the white-clad players on the green courts, a golf course blooming with dogwoods. That's why people come.

Soon at most county grounds, however, there will be no grass left outside the playing area. What is more pleasant than sitting on grass, or in a deckchair on grass, at the boundary, to watch a game played before you on grass? The image of the serrated jaw of a great digger gouging into a smooth lawn, its steel tracks having already ripped careless ruts and gashes across it, is especially painful.

As we've seen, at Canterbury over the last 20 years substantial tracts of grass have gone under ever more development. An aerial photograph of the St Lawrence Ground from as late as 1948 shows the glorious open parkland this once lovely ground used to be. Even the

Canterbury's St Lawrence Ground: open parkland as late as 1948.

playing area itself appears to have been shrunk to accommodate the newest development, as it has apparently at both Bristol and the Oval (though at Taunton, one of the most attractively improved grounds, it has actually been increased, to meet the minimum size to stage international matches).

At Hove, just as dismayingly, the traditional grassy bank at the Cromwell Road End – the deckchairs bank – was truncated a few years ago to make way for some glorified Portakabin offices. More is to come. In the latest Masterplan for the County Ground's redevelopment, 'A Vision for Sussex Cricket', the beer garden of the Sussex Cricketer pub at the Sea End, where I have enjoyed many delicious pints of Harvey's Best during luncheon intervals, looks set to disappear beneath a nine-storey block of flats. (The pub itself, 'a much-loved haunt for sports fans', was demolished in January 2021. *They knocked down a pub that sold Harvey's Best.* The report in the local paper, the *Argus*, was bylined 'Crime Reporter'.) And with a new permanent stand planned to stretch the full width of the Cromwell Road End that would seem to be the grassy bank gone for good.

There would appear to have been a certain pushback when the original plans were announced (and not just from me), so in the summer of 2021 the club's website was announcing that an effort will be made to retain 'the traditional village green feel of the club'. Among other things, 'the north-west and north-east corners will be lined with artificial grass for people to continue to be able to enjoy the afternoon sun on deckchairs.'

Then, after I thought I'd finished this chapter, I happened to go to Hastings. There, of course, at the end of the last century, the Central Recreation Ground, the historic town centre cricket ground surrounded by high Georgian houses where in 1947 Denis Compton broke Jack Hobbs' record by scoring 17 centuries in a season, disappeared under a shopping centre. The consolation prize offered was a new,

↑ The final County Championship game at the Central Recreation Ground, Hastings.
↓ Deckchairs on the grassy bank at Hove's Cromwell Road End.

state-of-the-art facility elsewhere in the town. But you would have hoped that the loss of cricket's Firestone Building had drawn a line in the sand – at least in Hastings. 'I'll take you to see the cricket ground my son's been playing at,' sighed the friend I'd gone to see when I told her about this book. 'They're going to build houses on it.'

It was a blazing sunny day, and off a leafy road just out of the town centre we came upon a vast lawn, a serene sea of green, bounded by mature trees all the way from scoreboard to pavilion. Into the attractive iron gates were wrought the initials 'HP'. Horntye Park. Wasn't this . . . the ground that only twenty years ago had justified the destruction of the North Marine Road of the South Coast?

A planning map HL21 on the Hastings Borough Council website revealed an 'indicative capacity' of no fewer than 250 houses. There was a proposal, it appeared, for the cricket club to be relocated, or marginalised, to the grounds of a closed prep school 20 minutes' drive away.

There is pressure from central government on councils to deliver thousands of new houses every year. Most of the time most people are just doing their best with a bad hand. But it is official government policy nowadays for playing fields not to be sold off. We have a climate crisis, an obesity crisis and a mental health crisis. Councils like Stockton-on-Tees and Nottingham now attach such importance to green space that they're exploring the idea of knocking down their redundant town centre shopping precincts to make way for . . . new parks.

Why is it always the cricket ground that gets it?

Horntye Park, Hastings: already under threat of housing development.

02

TREES

f I think of a cricket ground without trees what first comes to mind is an antiseptic stadium. Are there any at all these days at the modern Oval, capacious and T20- and conference-friendly though it may be? Even the olive trees in planters that in recent years stood near the Jack Hobbs Gates look set to be displaced by the Mound Stand redevelopment. Then again, North Marine Road in Scarborough doesn't have any that I can think of, and that's in its way one of the most picturesque places of all to watch cricket, especially with a big festival crowd in.

But nowhere ever suffered from becoming more sylvan, and it remains the case that trees only ever enhance a cricket ground. Consider the transformation of the County Ground in Northampton since the football club moved out: not just the smart indoor school at the Abington Avenue end with its wings of stands neatly framing the playing area at last, but the screen of purple-leaved Norway maples along the perimeter wall, felicitously matching the club's traditional maroon. They turn something previously utilitarian into a destination. (Northampton is also an excellent argument for all a cricket ground's plastic seating being white: not only is it in a clean harmony with the

North Marine Road, Scarborough: no trees, but still a wonderful ground, especially during the Cricket Festival.

players' clothing, but it also leaves nature to supply more than sufficient colour in all the surrounding trees' gradations of green, brown and red.)

Of course, all this has something to do with the implement we play the game with: a contoured, crafted, seasoned blade of English willow wood. Golf used to be played with a piece of hickory wood: now it's become a contest of titanium technologies. But even though these days cricket bats may be mighty clubs with names like the Powerbow Inferno and the Oblivion Stealth (I had no idea), designed to propel every top-edged swipe high into the stands, underneath all the decals and logos it's still a piece of tree. Bat-making itself remains something of a cottage industry: anyone, effectively, can become a supplier of willow timber for it: you just need your small patch of woodland. So in fact the game of cricket in the 21st century actually encourages afforestation and re-wilding.

When prosthetic limbs were still made of wood, fine-grained hard woods like oak, ash and lime were most commonly used for their man-ufacture, but this entry in *Carr's Dictionary of Extra-Ordinary Cricketers* appears to suggest that willow was used at least once:

The Revd Elisha Fawcett, c. 1817, a Manchester evangelical who devoted his life to teaching the natives of the Admiralty Islands the commandments of God and the Laws of Cricket. Too poor to purchase a monument to this good man, his parishioners erected his wooden leg upon his grave. In that fertile clime it miraculously took root and for many years provided a bountiful harvest of bats.

Purple-leafed cultivar of Norway maple at the County Ground, Northampton.

I'm not sure every entry in *Carr's Dictionary* comes across as entirely credible, and his *How Steeple Sinderby Wanderers Won the FA Cup* was of course pure fiction, but this is the West, sir. When the legend becomes fact, print the legend.

Trees play a number of crucial roles at cricket grounds: architectural, climatic, monumental and ornamental. In earlier times, of course, before the advent of cantilevered stands, they also offered an elevated vantage-point for watching the action. Of the Europeans versus Hindus match in the Bombay Quadrangular tournament of 1923 a reporter recorded that 'Every pavilion was full and hundreds were watching the game from house-tops, while some were perched on trees.'

Think of truly lovely grounds like Arundel Castle, created in 1895 by the 25th Duke of Norfolk, where Sussex have staged an annual festival since the historic Hastings ground was submerged under a shopping precinct, or Coldharbour up in the Surrey Hills, 'just a large smite away from Leith Hill', as Brian Levison puts it in *Remarkable Village Cricket Grounds*, and officially the highest ground in the south of England, or the little grounds tucked away at the extremities of Kew Gardens or Sheffield Park in Sussex. These are quite simply woodland clearings in which cricket is played. They are enfolded by trees: compact arboreal amphitheatres. Coming upon them is to feel you're standing alongside Walter de la Mare's traveller as his 'horse in the silence champed the grasses/ Of the forest's ferny floor': a magic and a wonder as this secret oasis opens out around you.

There may be longer breaks for lost balls at grounds like these, but the surrounding forest coming almost up to the boundary rope also seals them for ever, you would think, just as they are: no tempting corners of greensward to sell off to a developer – and in any case, the National Trust owns both Coldharbour and Sheffield Park, and the Royal Botanical Gardens Kew, so we're not going to see a Travelodge or a McCarthy & Stone at any of those.

Three forest clearings: ← Arundel Castle; → Sheffield Park; ↓ Coldharbour.

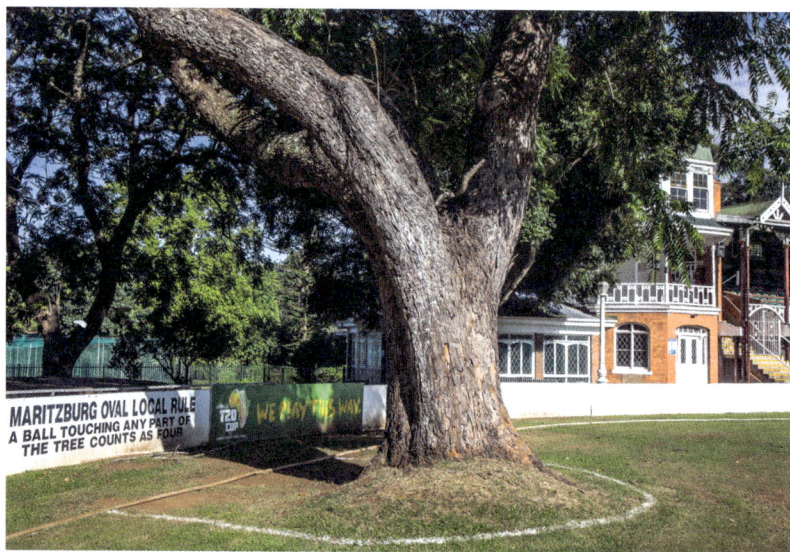

Trees inside the boundary: ↑ Pietermaritzburg, South Africa; ↓ the Canterbury lime (when it still was).

Occasionally (though only in the past), the game of cricket is so respectful of the prior tenure of a mature tree that it simply builds the entire ground around it. One such is at Pietermaritsburg in South Africa, another at Amstelveen in the Netherlands (who of course have beaten England twice in one-day internationals), and a third at the Sennoke ground in Kent, situated within the rolling parkland of the Knole estate at Sevenoaks.

But the famous example in Britain was at Kent's St Lawrence Ground in Canterbury – the most legendary cricket tree in the country apart from George Parr's Tree at Trent Bridge, an elm named after the nineteenth-century Nottinghamshire batsman who until the arrival of W.G. Grace was claimed to be the finest anywhere in the world (a bough was laid on his casket). Parr's elm stood just inside the boundary wall at the West Bridgford end for 170 years until it came down during gales at the start of 1976. 'Most cricket grounds are devoid of any trees or shrubs,' declares Wikipedia tendentiously: 'the St Lawrence Ground was an exception: when the ground opened in 1847 it was laid out around a pre-existing lime tree, which was then about 40 years old.'

At its tallest, by the late twentieth century it was 130 feet high, and two of only four cricketers to have cleared its crown were West Indians: Learie Constantine and Carl Hooper. But high winds brought the old tree down for good in 2005, and Jim Swanton planted its replacement sapling outside the playing area, which was moved to the site of its predecessor six years later. But since 2017 it's been beyond the boundary rope again, like any old tree, thanks to the encroachment of the new retirement flats. One wonders if Kent CCC would have dared, had the old, 200-year-old tree still been standing, but the defenestration of the Kent lime is a rather literal symbol of how the issue of trees at cricket grounds nowadays gets marginalised.

If your shot hit the Canterbury lime you got 4. In January 1999 the *Daily Telegraph*'s Letters page printed a contribution from Peter Kemp of Epsom headlined 'Beech Tree Rules' (subsequently collected

in *Not in My Day, Sir: Cricket Letters to the* Daily Telegraph), recalling 'a specimen copper beech tree at Welton Cricket Club, near Daventry'.

> During the Fifties, it was a 'local rule' that if a cricket ball was hit into the tree, the batsman could be dismissed if a fielder caught the ball red-handed.
>
> This was not always easy as the ball tended to ricochet from branch to branch on its way down and its emergence from the boughs could not be predicted until the last moment. Sometimes the ball would fall to the ground after a few seconds and elude more than one fieldsman, and it was often the chance for the batsmen to turn one run into two as the ball slowly came down.

Trees can also be planted to define the very boundary of a cricket ground: a felicitous arboreal alternative to the Oval's endless redbrick wall. On Clifton and Durdham Downs, in the west of Bristol, seven aged beech trees survive from the 16 planted back in the mid-nineteenth century to demarcate the first county ground for the newly inaugurated Gloucestershire County Cricket Club – with the great W. G. Grace instrumental in the foundation of both. Most of the trees have been aged back to around 1867, which tallies with the first county match there taking place in 1870 (as you'd expect, Grace's team won).

← Bristol's boundary beeches on Clifton and Durdham Downs.
→ Rockingham's magnificent poplars in Northamptonshire.

One of the most picturesque architectural components for a cricket ground is a row of Lombardy poplars, or plantière poplars to give the UK variant we usually have in the UK its proper name. Crondall and the eponymous Poplars in Nottinghamshire are two striking examples, and Rockingham in Northants a sensational third. Naturally riparian trees, with their slender fastigiate form (branches growing upwards in champagne-flute shape), poplars bring a natural colonnade to a cricket ground.

But their contribution is more than aesthetic or demarcatory: they are planted as shelter belts: as windbreaks to shield against sweeping gusts that could make a game unplayable. In more gentler breezes they'll also rustle in a delightful susurrus. I think cricket clubs should plant them as ubiquitously as the French do along their country roads.

As the Canterbury lime, shows, though, trees aren't always a guarantor against development, and the counties' record on poplars is not great. Taunton had a line of them along the River Tone side of the ground – but more retirement flats as part of a new stand built in 2009 now tower where the trees once did. I'd quite like to retire to live beside a cricket ground – but I'd like to *look out on trees*. Headingley used to have a handsome line of poplars as well, at the Kirkstall Lane End: you can see them still there in the footage of Botham's 1981 Ashes heroics. But now Headingley is a stadium, not a ground, and I can't see any poplars around that giant new Carnegie Pavilion.

My aspens dear, whose airy cages quelled,
Quelled or quenched in leaves the leaping sun,
  All felled, felled, are all felled;
  Of a fresh and following folded rank
    Not spared, not one
    That dandled a sandalled
   Shadow that swam or sank
On meadow and river and wind-wandering weed-winding bank.

'O if we knew but what we do,' continues Gerard Manley Hopkins in 'Binsey Poplars', 'When we delve or hew – /Hack and rack the growing green!' In the zero-sum contest between green space and development green space is not yet winning, and not only when it comes to cricket stadia, but when we think of climate change and the quality of our air, never mind the peace of our souls, we already know it has to one day, don't we? I guess I don't understand why, at least when it comes to cricket, and where it's played, we don't *want* to go green – even more than we are already . . .

If the rejoinder is that we now have to cater for the short-attention-span instant-gratification slogfest audience that will pack out the Oval every night, well, ever since my father, a good club cricketer with the distinguished Alexandra Park club, threw a cooking apple from our lawn over the poplar trees at the end of our garden because my sister and I had dared him to, I have seen poplars as a glove thrown down

Boycott's hundredth 100 at Headingley in 1977, framed by the Kirkstall Lane End poplars.

for a six hit. Never mind 'the second level of the stand': see if you can smack it over them! I'd tune in to the Hundred for that.

In other words trees, at county grounds, often seem to be treated as just in the way. Part of the pleasure of going down to Hove for the first County Championship match of the season in April was to be greeted, as you came in through the gates at the Sea End, past the beer garden of the Sussex Cricketer with its shade trees to sit under, by the magnificent magnolia laden with voluptuous pink blossom. It announces in its entirely natural, beautiful way, that the season – and not only the cricket season, but also the new life of the whole spring unfurling in fresh leaves and tender buds – is awakening at last. I assume it will survive the latest ground redevelopment, but I can't see it on the plans.

If we look at the most recent new-build county headquarters, the Rose Bowl in Southampton (well, West End, since it's nowhere near the actual city of Southampton), opened in 2001, the arboreal audit is mixed. It was previously farmland, so a large portion of green space has now been covered in buildings, access roads, car parks and stands. Its bowl-shaped design makes it definitely a stadium, not a cricket ground, but around the perimeter of the stands has been planted a ring of what look like field maples, which are now coming into maturity and hang a decorous green curtain behind the rather arid, beige banking of plastic seats. On the other hand, the pavilion, when first constructed, had not only Telegraph Woods as its backdrop but also an undeniably stirring prospect from its upper tiers of the deep green quilt of forest beyond the M27 – until they went and stuck a great long barracks of a hotel at the far end of the ground to block it out entirely.

Lord's, though, has always been an exception. Even after having been almost completely reconstructed since the Seventies, with its magnificent mature plane trees at both ends it has remained a true cricket ground, not a stadium. When the original Compton and Edrich stands at the Nursery End were built at the end of the Eighties, indeed,

Lieutenant-Colonel John Stephenson, the then secretary of the MCC (which owns and is therefore responsible for the redevelopment of the ground), was interviewed during the BBC's Test coverage explaining why their overall height had to be restricted specifically so that the view of the plane trees behind not be obscured. Lord's is, after all, within the St John's Wood Conservation Area, 'a leafy and relatively low-density residential suburb', in the words of Westminster Council.

But now, after only 30 years, these original Compton and Edrich Stands have already come down, to be replaced by, at the apex, the highest stands in the ground, in order to accommodate 2,500 more seats and, perhaps more importantly, more restaurant/hospitality suite facilities. To achieve all that the new stand's footprint has to be larger, which in turn means that, in order to preserve the dimensions of the existing Nursery ground (I quote from now on from Westminster Council's planning officer's report, available online),

> Eleven mature London plane trees and one mature horse
> chestnut tree are proposed to be removed to facilitate
> the development. The majority of the trees are protected
> by virtue of a tree preservation order, the remainder
> are protected by virtue of being with St John's Wood
> Conservation Area. The applicant has proposed replacement
> planting including five *Celtis australis* trees planted in the
> ground and four multi stemmed *Celtis australis* trees planted
> outside the site boundary planted in pots.

Celtis australis, by the way, is a little nettle tree: fine for a suburban street where you don't want a leviathan lifting the pavement and blocking households' light, but hardly a substitute for a grand London plane – and four of these would appear to be just little lollipops stuck in pots outside the ground.

No wonder, then, that the council's tree officer or Arboricultural

Manager (every borough has one, responsible for the planting and maintenance and oversight of all its trees, be they in streets, parks or on private property)

has objected to the proposal on the grounds of the loss of these trees and inadequate tree planting and landscaping. The Arboricultural Manager has stated that proposed replacement trees do not have a good form, and will not reach a stature equivalent to the London planes, so would never replace the amenity that the existing trees provided. The trees which are proposed in pots would be short-lived, and shrubby in habit, and would not make any meaningful landscape contribution. The size of the proposed stands are such that large growing trees are necessary to offset the scale of the development. London plane trees are typical

These perambulating spectators' view of plane trees at Lord's Nursery End has been abolished by the towering new stands.

of the area and are tolerant of the likely difficult growing environment and would be a superior choice . . . The Arboricultural Manager has suggested that a section 106 contribution to tree planting offsite is sought for no less than £50,000

– in other words, that Lord's make a contribution of £50,000 to finance the planting of equivalent trees elsewhere in the borough to mitigate the loss of all these magnificent mature (and protected) planes and horse chestnut. However, according to the report, 'The applicant has declined to make a financial contribution to enable replacement provision outside of the site', but does state

that as part of the Lord's masterplan, additional tree-planting is proposed adjacent to the south-eastern edge of the Nursery Pitch. Although it is acknowledged that these trees do not form part of this planning submission, they are a key aspect of the Lord's masterplan which MCC have a proven track record of delivering . . . the additional tree provision within the wider site . . . will . . . provide suitable mitigation for the short-term loss of trees . . . The total number of trees will exceed the current provision in a manner that will allow the development and growth of the ground.

So, concludes the council's report, though 'It is most regrettable that 12 mature trees are to be lost . . . the proposal as a whole will involve substantial other public benefits and for that reason on balance it is not considered that the proposal should be refused because of the loss of the trees.'

But that is how cricket loses a little more of its nature.

03

FLOWERS, PLANTS AND SHRUBS

'Bumble bees on the clover at third man,' reflects Mike Jones of the Wildlife Trusts: 'used to keep me occupied for hours . . .'

There is not supposed to be anything other than grass on a cricket field. Nowadays, you would only expect to find plants and flowers beyond a boundary, and those predominantly horticultural. Hanging baskets are, of course, a fixture on many cricket pavilions and even modern hospitality facilities – the Point at Old Trafford is a futuristic example. At Grace Road, the homely headquarters of Leicestershire CCC, they even have a traditional flower bed of roses and the like in front of the pavilion. Rhododendrons have become invasive in the wild nowadays to the extent that parties descend on Lake District slopes for a spot of what is still for some reason celebrated as 'rho-do-bashing', but as a purple and pink backdrop to the Nevill Ground at Tunbridge Wells, where Kent still play a decorous festival at the beginning of June, they are stunning. 'No ground in England more resembles a tropical greenhouse,' wrote Alan Ross.

We have to go back to Edwardian times, or at least before the last war, for a cricket field itself that could be celebrated in today's biodiversity surveys as 'species-rich'. Here is the ground at Fordenden in Kent that greets A. G. Macdonell's hero Donald in *England, Their England* as he arrives from London:

> The cricket field itself was a mass of daisies and buttercups and dandelions, tall grasses and purple vetches and thistle-down, and great clumps of dark-red sorrel, except, of course, for the oblong patch in the centre – mown, rolled, watered – a smooth, shining emerald of grass, the Pride of Fordenden, the wicket.

(Who, these days, would even be able to put names to all these wild flowers?)

Pre-war games on outfields that saw a scythe once or twice a year

← Hanging baskets at the Point, Old Trafford; → flower bed at Grace Road, Leicester; ↓ rhododendrons at the Nevill Ground, Tunbridge Wells.

if they were lucky may have pre-determined low totals, but if you did connect sweetly, according to *Carr's Dictionary of Extra-Ordinary Cricketers*, even weeds could could compile a century.

> George Thwaites, c. 1923, playing in a Monk Fryston meadow, hit a ball into a thick clump of nettles, locally notorious for their fierce sting and subsequently bitter and long-lasting rash. Although lost ball was called, the batsman deviated from his course between the pitched stumps to point out first the ball and then the Unalterable Law that thus it could not be a lost ball. He then returned to complete 189 self-counted runs before a fielder's father fetched his scythe.

Species-rich unimproved limestone grassland at Crickley Hill SSSI, Gloucestershire.

There is still a place for wild flora at cricket grounds, however. The Gloucestershire Wildlife Trust manages a reserve at Crickley Hill that is an SSSI (Site of Special Scientific Interest) for both its ancient woodland and its unimproved limestone grassland – 'Forty per cent of the Cotswolds used to be covered in it,' explains Gareth Parry, the Trust's Director for Nature's Recovery. 'Now there's only one per cent left.' If you leave such grassland alone, it is astonishingly species-rich: 'There's literally hundreds of plants you'd find – bellflower, horseshoe vetch, black and greater knapweed – hundreds of invertebrates, hundreds of moths and butterflies like Small Blues . . .'

The cricket ground next door, though – Bharat Cricket Club, an old-established and traditional club – is excluded from the SSSI, as you'd rather expect. Here is the essential conflict of interest between a cricket ground and a nature reserve. A ground that's regularly mown as short as a cricket outfield, says Gareth,

it's a bonsai-ed version of the unimproved grassland. Anywhere they stopped cutting it, it would grow as species-rich grassland. CG-5 grassland [the technical term for the unimproved sort] we don't mow between May and the first weeks of July. You do need to cut it, as otherwise the grasses will take over: wildflowers flourish when nutrients are really low, like on limestone grassland.

You can see the problem with not mowing a cricket ground at all between May and July . . .

Bee orchid on the boundary at Pleshey CC, Essex.

But Gareth points to a felicitous compromise. In the nearby Cotswold village of Oakridge Lynch, the cricket club is fortunate to have a particularly large playing area, 'to such an extent that beyond the boundaries there's a band about ten metres wide – we'd like it to be bigger – where they've let it grow long.' The difference in biodiversity, he explains, is huge: 20 to 30 plants per square metre in the uncut verge; four to five on the mown outfield, which is effectively just rye grass and clover. 'And the more plants, the more birds, bees, insects . . . The difference between insect populations is absolutely huge.'

Perhaps the club ground Mike Jones played on was a village green, and therefore a community asset with multiple uses beyond summer cricket. The village green at Lurgashall in Sussex, on which cricket is also played, is, notes Clare Blencowe of the Sussex Wildlife Trust, important for the presence of chamomile. Chamomile has become much rarer across the country, even in the South and South-west where it's now principally found. It's apparently pretty much died

Red ginger or teuila (the Samoan national flower), yellow heliconia and banana trees at the Mauga village cricket ground.

Living walls: ↑ the new Warner Stand at Lord's; ↓ the OCS Stand at the Oval.

out on the heathland commons where it was traditionally found, but it survives best on sward that's grazed and trampled by cattle, so grass that's kept short by mowing, as on the outfield of cricket pitches, will do just as well.

In urban areas, however, where 'built-up' these days means literally up, a recent trend in 'greening' the environment is the 'living wall': covering the vertical outside wall of a building with vegetation. Homeowners have long done this unofficially by trailing wisteria up the outside of their houses, but of course that flowers but once and briefly during the year. The idea of living walls is that they're green all year round, for which you need an intricate and expensive irrigation system, which of course doesn't always work properly. 'I've seen them dying all over London,' sighed a friend. Pumping water up a vertical wall also requires energy, which is not necessarily green. And living walls can be proposed by developers as a mitigating expedient when their plans involve the destruction of other natural things like trees, or at least a more intensive development than was there before.

But London's two biggest cricket grounds have both gone in for green walls in recent years: the Oval with its huge OCS stand at the Vauxhall End in 2005, and Lord's most recently on the side of its new Warner Stand. The planting there, by the consultancy Biotecture, mixes a number of familiar plants – all evergreen, as you'd expect – often used in garden design to give maximum ground coverage, like euonymus, sedge grass, ivy and pachysandra, a glossy-leaved plant with white flowers. Here, however, they need to clump and spread vertically, for which specific small-leaved cultivars seem to have been selected. Lirope, a purple-flowered plant, likes shade: useful when the wall it's on is in a kind of canyon caused by the stand's high sides. It seems to me you're likely to see a living wall when all the ground that could have had a tree planted or a garden laid out on it has been built on, but it's better than looking up at concrete or cladding.

04

FUNGI

A number of the more bucolic village cricket grounds in Britain adjoin SSSIs (officially designated Sites of Special Scientific Interest) or LWSs (Local Wildlife Sites). In addition to Bharat in the Cotswolds, as we saw in Chapter 3, examples include Rufford and the lovely White Coppice in Lancashire, and Harpenden Common and Chipperfield Common in Hertfordshire. But non-designation certainly doesn't rule out real ecological significance, as the North West Fungus Group discovered in 2017.

The Group organises regular 'forays' (outings to particular sites to survey their fungus populations), and in 2015 Philip Sinclair, the secretary and groundsman, 'as well as numerous other roles', of Kirby Lonsdale Cricket Club in Cumbria joined one led by members Mike and Di Hall. A year later Mike got a call from Phil to say he'd found a purple coral on the outfield and, after consulting his field guide, thought it was probably *Clavaria zollingeri*. Of any interest?

'The next day', writes Mike in his report in the NWFG's Spring 2017 newsletter, whose masthead features a colour photograph of a large chocolate birthday cake adorned with colourful, and one hopes sugar, toadstools,

> Di and I went down to take a look and were quite taken aback with what we saw — quite 'bowled over'. The entire outfield was covered in fungi numbering thousands. The vast majority were waxcaps. He was right about the *C. Zollingeri* and in a walk round the outfield we counted over 120 clumps. We also spotted species of *Trichoglossum* and *Geoglossum*, various spindles and other grassland associates.

The next day, on another foray on Ingleborough, they ran into a Natural England mycologist (an expert on fungi) called Andy McLay, a specialist in waxcaps. He got down to the cricket ground the day after that. Mike Hall quotes from his subsequent email:

I've been surveying waxcap grasslands for over 20 years now and I have to say that this site is one of the very best that I have seen. The score to date of 18 waxcaps, 6 fairy clubs and 3 earthtongue species would easily qualify the site as 'eligible for consideration as an SSSI'. The single visit count of 17 waxcap species would also suggest that the field is of international importance for this group. In my experience their presence together with Clavaria zollingeri, *Microglossum olivaceum*, *Geoglossum atropurpureum*, *Hygrocybe ovina*, *H.nitrata* and *H. punicea* absolutely confirms this.

Kirkby Lonsdale CC's fungi: ↑ crimson waxcaps (*Hygrocybe punicea*); ← purple coral (*Clavaria zollingeri*); → a cluster of white spindles (*Clavaria fragilis*).

For the record, here is the full alphabetical list of waxcap species recorded on Kirby Lonsdale's outfield in 2017:

Hygrocybe calyptriformis, H. Ceracea, H. Chlorophana, H. citrinovirens H. Cuccinea, H. conica var. Conica, H. flavipes, H. Fornicata, H. Intermedia, H. Irrigata, H. Nitrata, H. Ovina, H. Pratensis, H. Psittacina, H. Punicea, H. Quieta, H. Reidii, H. virginea

And the other fungi found there:

Clavaria fragilis, Clavulinopsis corniculata, Clavulinopsis helvola, Cordyceps militaris, Mycena adonis, Cystoderma amianthinum, and two common *Rickenella sp.*

So why, as Mike Hall reasonably asks, would a non-SSSI like Kirby Lonsdale Cricket Club be such a mycological mecca, particularly since 'the fields around it are rank grass grazed by sheep and are virtually devoid of fungi'? The answer is, he explains, that the ground is situated just north of Devil's Bridge over the River Lune, and

> the pitch has been fenced off for over 70 years. It has never
> been fertilised and is just cut short during the cricket
> season. But there is more to it than that. Most of the Kirby
> Lonsdale area is Silurian shale or boulder clay, but there
> is a tongue of carboniferous limestone underlaying the
> River Lune and the cricket pitch at this point. So we have
> unimproved, short grassland overlaying limestone – perfect!

In other words, the same unimproved limestone grassland as would harbour an abundance of wild flowers.

Follow the nearby Settle and Carlisle railway line down to Leeds, however, and a fungus has gone down in notoriety in cricket history.

At Headingley in 1972 it was 'The fungus that floored the Aussies', as Martin Williamson's feature for espncricinfo.com is dramatically headlined.

After three Tests the home Ashes series against Ian Chappell's Australians was all square at one-all, meaning the Aussies needed to win both of the remaining two to re-take the Ashes. A youthful Dennis Lillee was looking forward to the bouncy, green wickets you could usually expect at Headingley, where swing bowling really came into its own. But the Australians arrived at the ground to find a wicket on which the ball would barely bounce at all. 'It has been completely shaven of grass,' fulminated the former Australian cricketer Jack Fingleton in *The Times*. 'Far too much has been taken off.' Coincidentally,

'Deadly' Derek Underwood traps Greg Chappell LBW in the 'fusarium Test' at Headingley in 1972.

England had picked two spinners: Ray Illingworth, the captain, and 'Deadly' Derek Underwood.

There was an innocent explanation, it was subsequently protested. There had been prolonged rain at Headingley in the run-up to the match – hardly unheard-of – and while the covers had been on, a fungus called fusarium had got in underneath and killed all the grass before the groundstaff had noticed.

Fusarium nivale, now called *Microdochium nivale*, more commonly fusarium patch or snow mould (because it often attacks lawns or golf course greens after snow thaws), is, in the Royal Horticultural Society's words, 'one of the most damaging diseases of turf grasses and can be difficult to control'. First of all small patches of grass go yellow, then brown, and die; then they grow larger and join up. Greg Chappell, however, observed how 'It was uncanny that it only attacked a strip 22 yards by eight feet, and the rest of the ground was perfectly healthy.' On the adjacent strip the ball came off at chest height.

Anyway, after lunch on the first afternoon 'Deadly' got wheeling away and Australia lost five wickets in 40 minutes and crashed to 98–7, eventually being bowled out for 146. When it was the Aussies' turn to bowl, 'The couple of times I tried to bowl a bouncer, I was embarrassed by the result,' admitted Dennis Lillee. On a pitch so slow England didn't find batting much easier, but they still got a first innings lead of over a hundred, and when 'Deadly' took another six wickets in the Australians' second innings to finish with 10 for the match, England were left with only 20 to get.

Afterwards the Australians were tight-lipped, though apparently their manager grumbled that they'd been 'dudded'. Derek Underwood put the win down to the hard work of the England bowlers. A wicket is the same for both sides: he was unquestionably the best spinner. The final Test of the series was at the Oval – in those days always a really fast, dry pitch. This time, in the comfortable Australian victory, after the Ashes had gone, it was Dennis Lillee who took 10 wickets.

05

GEOLOGY

The easiest way to understand the relevance of geological factors to cricket is to look at some photos.

Would Newlands in Cape Town be the same ground without Table Mountain? Or Dharamshala without the Indian Himalayas? Or Sedbergh School, in Cumbria, without the Howgills?

By geology we mean the very rocks out of which this solid sphere to which we cling is made – sometimes rupturing and rearing up as a result of stupendous tectonic forces into the mountain ranges of today, sometimes broken down into the friable soil in which things grow.

There is a geological reason, in other words, why captains at the historic St Helen's ground in Swansea check the tide table before the toss. St Helen's is built on a reclaimed sandbank. It would have to be sand, because St Helen's is right next to the sea, and sand is rock that has been scoured over aeons by the ceaseless motion of the waves into the fine granules we associate with going to the beach. The tide in Mumbles Bay goes out more than a quarter of a mile, which makes the sandy subsoil of the cricket field dry out at low tide as quickly as anywhere in the country. But when the tide comes in, the subsoil absorbs underground moisture just as fast, and if you've got swing bowlers in your team when it's going to be high tide, then if you win the toss you want to be putting the other side in.

I am not a geologist, or even a scientist at all, and I confess that detailed explanations of how mountain ranges came to be over vast epochs of prehistoric time leave me cold: ultimately the thing about a rock is that it is just *there* and, unlike an evanescent dragonfly or cherry blossom, it's not going away, or indeed anywhere. So however Table Mountain came to be Table Mountain – how the erosion of a superior but softer layer of rock over thousands of years left the flat table-top or *mesa* of the hard granitic sandstone beneath that dominates the city of Cape Town today – *it's over*, OK? But what do such vast outcrops of rock do for a cricket ground?

↑ St Helen's, Swansea: bowl when the tide's coming in.
↓ England play at Queenstown Oval, Otago, New Zealand.

Pretty much all other sports stadia are inward-looking: the playing areas are a lot smaller anyway, which, with the encircling stands
closing in, only increases the introversion, but the effect, even the
aim, is to create the concentrated atmosphere of the cockpit. Cricket,
on the other hand, is always open to the heavens. There should always
be a sky above as wide as Montana's. We should always be able to see
the horizon. We're always looking beyond the boundary. So, far from
being a claustrophobic, looming presence, the montane panorama of
the Himalayas, or even Winder fell looking down on Sedbergh, forces

Table Mountain dominates the Newlands ground in Cape Town, South Africa.

us to look up – to spectate in three dimensions. That's why I don't want to see a six just plopping into the third tier of some grandstand – that actually diminishes the enterprise. I want to see that ball soaring into the empyrean like a peregrine.

But also, isn't cricket a magnificently strange game? Look at little Lynton and Lynmouth Cricket Club, hung inside the awesome sweep of the Valley of the Rocks on the Devon coast. Isn't this a location for *The Lord of the Rings* rather than a village cricket ground, and just as otherworldly for either? There are feral goats wandering over this landscape, and also white-clad cricketers. And don't these colossal rock edifices dwarfing a little cricket match beneath also console us that this game is ultimately of less than cosmic import, even whimsical

and transient in nature, just as the circled covered wagons of football stands encourage the delusion that soccer really is much more than a matter of life and death? 'Yes, it's Test cricket,' reflected a rueful Cameron Bancroft in a recent interview with the *Guardian*'s Donald McRae of his involvement in the Australian ball-tampering episode. 'Yes, it's something to be really proud of. But it is just a game.'

And while we're on *The Lord of the Rings*, there is the legend of Mežica Cricket Club in Slovenia, on the mountainous border with Austria, which has literally come out of the earth. For 300 years human beings mined for lead and zinc inside Mount Peca, a sacred mountain inside which slumbers King Mathew, as he has been doing ever since he escaped from the Turks. Once his beard has grown nine times round the table (presumably on which he fell asleep), he will wake up and there will be justice and peace on Earth.

Lancashire play county cricket at Sedbergh School in the shadow of Winder in the Howgill Fells.

Meanwhile in 1974 a 14-year-old schoolboy called Borut Cegovnik from the nearby mining town of Mežica went on an English exchange to Kent, where he stayed with the family of a coal salesman called Charles Nest, who was also the single-wicket champion of Birchington-on-Sea Cricket Club. Fired with fascination for this weird but compelling English ritual, Borut returned to Slovenia and, with much consultation of the MCC's Rules of Cricket, got the game of cricket going in his town, while King Mathew slept on. In 1994 the mine finally closed, and the site was reclaimed and landscaped, and the meadow where Mežica CC originally played was covered with a supermarket, and King Mathew slept on.

So on the doorstep of the old mine the club created this fabulous ground: a kind of Slovenian Wormsley, or indeed a 'Balkan Lord's', as its members sometimes refer to it, that hosts matches in the

Lynton and Lynmouth's stunning ground in the Valley of the Rocks on the north Devon coast.

three-team Slovenian league and visiting sides from countries like Serbia. 'It's the most picturesque ground I have ever played on,' Jonathan Campion told me – he went there in 2014 during a cricket tour of the Balkans with Carmel and District CC from North Wales. 'It is also the only ground where my skiddy slow-mediums have been hit to all parts by a former Winter Olympic ski jumper.' Birchington-on-Sea CC, on the other hand, has since folded, and Birchington is currently without a cricket ground. Wake up, King Mathew!

Mežica CC's ground in the Slovenian mountains on land reclaimed from the old lead and zinc mine.

06

BACK TO NATURE:
The Abandoned Cricket Ground

The last ball feathers the edge, thuds into the wicket-keeper's gloves and is tossed high – or perhaps speeds to the extra-cover boundary. The umpire lifts the bails, the players shake hands and walk off to the pavilion. Soon, as the last car drives off, the ground is deserted, and that's it for the season.

But come next April the grass is still growing. By the September it is calf-high. A pavilion window is cracked. Bird droppings spatter the heavy roller, and the odd spot of rust. By Christmas there are dandelions and dock leaves and even a sycamore sapling poking up in the outfield.

Perhaps the club couldn't get enough players together to raise a side. Perhaps the long-serving captain-cum-secretary-cum-groundsman-cum odd-job man who had run everything finally retired to the coast. Perhaps the landowner refused to renew the lease, with an eye to a nice little development of 'heritage' houses. Whatever: no more cricket here. Play has been abandoned. Maybe for ever.

But of course life – Life – goes on. The natural world doesn't realise this is supposed to be a picturesque cricket ground. Trees throw out spores. Birds drop seeds. Bees buzz from stamen to stamen. The rain falls. The sun shines. The grass grows.

Indeed, it is when you visit, or even just look at a picture of, an abandoned cricket ground that you realise what a neat, orderly, meticulous game this is. I remember rugby league matches on TV fought out on pitches that looked as though they'd already been turned over by pigs. On links courses in Scotland hacking your errant ball out of thickets of heather and gorse is one of golf's most supreme challenges. But cricket never runs riot. Now look at Highbury in Yorkshire in 2009, though, just five years after its last game, which brought to an end nearly 80 years of history, and almost 60 playing in the Leeds League, at its little ground on the edge of Meanwood Park 'with its tree-lined boundaries completely surrounded by streams', as it was

celebrated as late as 1992 in the commemorative handbook for the
League's centenary. Highbury Cricket Club was praised for 'the excel-
lence of its playing surface': it still would be, as you'd imagine with the
irrigation of all that water flowing round it – but now by grasshoppers,
bees, butterflies and insectivorous birds.

Highbury CC in Yorkshire: ↑ a large crowd in back in 1957;
↓ already a wilderness in 2009, five years after the last game.

Staveley in Cumbria: ↑ Frank Monks and the Don behold a wild-flower meadow, 2011; ← Don Mounsey's watercolour evokes playing days.

Staveley in the Lake District, on the other hand, which I visited back in 2011, had been built on a former rubbish tip and, according to Frank Monks, who used to keep wicket for the club and took me down there, was never easy for batting, though that hadn't stopped Keith Donoghue, 'the Don', who joined us there and was still batting for Kendall 3rds at the age of 73, from being the best batsman in the Westmorland League and regularly tonking sixes into the river, which meant a lengthy expedition for the small boy dispatched to retrieve the ball because the bridge over it was half a mile away.

The club had been ejected from its ground here on Back Lane 20 years earlier because the factory next door, whose construction had previously annexed a fair bit of what had once been quite a large playing surface, wanted to expand, and the loss of its home saw it fold altogether. Staveley's location in a National Park had prevented planning permission, the factory had since closed, but the ground was still padlocked. 'What a waste', mused Frank and the Don, as they looked out towards the wicket. Never mind the quality of the original soil: twenty years of nature being left to its own devices had seen the square grow thick with meadow buttercups. If this was agricultural land a farmer would have received a nice emolument for the good deed of turning it into 'set-aside'. If it wouldn't have been better as a cricket field you could now call it a wild flower meadow.

Peter Gillman used to play for the *Sunday Times* team at the Times Newspapers sports club at Ravensbourne in Kent. There's quite an enclave of sports grounds in this leafy part of Beckenham: Millwall have their training ground next door, Crystal Palace's is not far away, and several survive of what used to be a number of works grounds, with Lloyds Bank's now Kent CCC's satellite ground hosting occasional county matches, and HSBC's beyond that.

But not the Ravensbourne cricket ground. After Times Newspapers was taken over by News International sports activities ceased when it was sold off to a property company. The 'magnificent pavilion'

Peter Gillman remembers was demolished, but again the developers had underestimated local planners' determination not to see priceless urban green space built over. Abutting the ground's eastern edge is what was then a golf course and is now, since 2019, Beckenham Place Park, 237 acres of rolling parkland and woodland that Lewisham Council has opened for public use, and will come to be treasured as South London's answer to Hampstead Heath. The ground, adjoining the park's southern edge, has become an unofficial addition to it, and quite right too.

It was on one of his lockdown walks through Beckenham Place Park in March 2021 that Peter Gillman, formerly of the *Sunday Times*'s peerless Insight team of investigative journalists, came upon his old sports ground 'in its present sorry state', a muddy dogwalkers' track crossing the square 'once so lovingly tended. The one remaining relic of those idyllic summer days is the rusting heavy roller I found in the undergrowth.' But the melancholy photographs Peter circulated among all his erstwhile *Sunday Times* team-mates evoked plenty of memories. 'Ah, I remember it well,' recalled Peter Watson, an Insight team colleague:

> In particular the time we were playing *Private Eye* and I was batting at number nine (having opened the bowling, I might add), and was out first ball, the middle one in a Michael Cockerell hat-trick. As I reached the pavilion, Mark Boxer, captain, opening bat, having knocked an elegant 22, and now turned scorer, without even looking up, quietly remarked, 'A little high up the order, I think, Peter.'

These were stellar contests: a distinguished BBC investigative journalist taking three wickets; one of the finest cartoonists of modern times opening the batting . . .

In another game, against the *Telegraph*, Will Ellsworth-Jones

(chief reporter, New York correspondent) was umpiring for a few overs, and found himself having to swallow hard and call the bowler, the *Telegraph*'s celebrated cricket correspondent (the former Glamorgan and MCC tour captain Tony Lewis), for a no-ball. On what grounds, inquired the bowler politely? Will explained the over-stepping, only to be told that the law had recently been changed by an MCC committee, chairman A. R. Lewis.

One evening in May, in the company of my friend Mathew Frith of the London Wildlife Trust, I paid the old *Times* ground a visit.

Already it was a very different sight from the place Peter Gillman had photographed: those hazy skeletons of trees around the perimeter had burst into thick, glowing green, and the ground, it was clear, was bounded by a lovely line of Lombardy poplars on its eastern boundary, and an equally fine procession of limes on the western. 'You've got a great poplar here, Graham,' Mathew was saying as we waded through the brambles and nettles at the southern end – 'a massive black poplar hybrid' (a sycamore, inevitably, had grown up in front of it). 'There's another . . . another . . . there's a line of them all the way through . . .' Then we found a fabulous, muscle-trunked field maple – it must have been a lovely spot to sit under and spectate – that Mathew thought at least a hundred years old. This ground, you could still partly see, had been arboreally laid out and defined – that was how it used to be done – as a green-walled arena. Suddenly I wished myself one of those superannuated rock stars occasionally filmed reclining in a hospitality box at a Lord's Test, able to snap my fingers and say, 'Buy it – just get

The Ravensbourne Times ground's old roller, discovered by Peter Gillman in March 2021.

it: find the plans of that pavilion and let's put the whole thing back again, just as it was . . .'

But the playing area now . . . 'It's quite eutrophic,' Mathew was musing – nitrogen-rich: 'there's stuff been dumped here. It's quite species-rich. This looks like Canadian goldenrod . . . nipplewort, goosegrass – these are all very typical disturbed-ground species.' Indeed: the outfield was no longer flat, but scrambly dunes, its humps already greened with grass and hogweed and creeping thistles. Mathew was pointing over at one of these hillocks: 'Blackcap – feeding on the mugwort and the flowers of the docks.' He bent down to a pretty little reddy-pink flower: 'cut-leaved cranesbill'. Suddenly you'd come upon a sandy, scrubby patch: no argument: the hardcore and shingle of builders' rubble. This forgotten field had become a useful repository for all the old stuff people had wanted forgotten about. But for Mathew the patches that were more interesting – where he was finding

By May the boundary trees have come into leaf, but a muddy dogwalkers' path still marches across the old square.

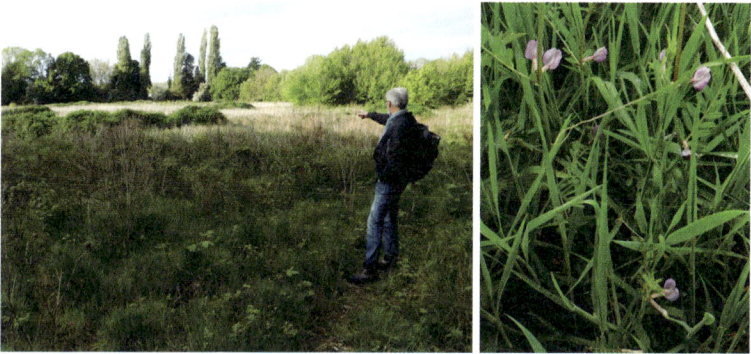

St John's wort, ribwort plantain, bristly oxtongue – were 'where the soil's been pushed around.' There were wrens singing; a chiffchaff was calling; a buff-tailed bumblebee was bumbling about.

And this was because nature just grew over everything that had been done to the old cricket field; had let nothing get in its way. Everything could be a habitat for something. 'You've got fantastic aspens, here, Graham!' (We were just inside the boundary from the hybrid poplars.) 'A whole copse! That'll get bigger over time. They're marching into the field.'

It was just after 7, and a lovely evening sun had come out: the kind of time a summer cricket match would just have been drawing to a close. 'When they last played here they wouldn't have had the parakeets,' said Mathew, as another screamed overhead. 'Those jackdaws as well': they'd been an almost entirely rural bird back then – 'the only colony would have been Richmond Park. Everything's so late this year,' he went on. 'In a month this is going to look fantastic.' But of the old roller Peter Gillman had come upon back in March when the trees were still bare: no sign, though we searched all over. Nature had reclaimed it for another year.

← Mathew Frith points out a blackcap singing; poplars beyond.
→ The pink flowers of common vetch on the old outfield.

But what happens if you *decide* to turn a cricket ground not into a block of flats, but something else natural? A couple of years ago the London Borough of Hackney's tree officer, Rupert Bentley Walls, proudly told me that some years earlier he'd planted lots of trees 'on an old cricket pitch down at Hackney Wick'. Normally this would be a hanging offence, but his subsequent achievement of turning the streets of Hackney into an urban arboretum by planting them with every conceivable species from persimmon to pecan is accepted in mitigation. The site was now called Wick Woodland, on the River Lea between the Olympic Park and the acres of football pitches on Hackney Marshes, so one evening a month into the 2021 cricket season I took Paul Wood, author of *London's Street Trees* and *London Tree Walks* and recently acclaimed as 'perhaps the best London tree navigator in the world', with me on a cricket archaeological expedition.

The entrance from the River Lea is, as you'll see, hardly on a par with the Grace Gates, especially with the nearby thunder of the A12 Blackwall Tunnel link, but along the wood's riverside boundary Paul and I found ourselves walking down an extraordinary avenue of over-arching London planes still to come into leaf. It was like being inside the ribcage of a blue whale. 'The old concrete wicket's still there in the middle,' Rupert had told me, but Paul was already murmuring about 'finding a needle in a haystack…'

Originally this tract of land would have been marshes, and therefore particularly low-lying, but apparently it had effectively been reclaimed during and immediately after the war when it was used as a dumping ground for rubble from buildings destroyed by bomb damage. 'That would have changed the geology quite a bit,' said Paul. The woodland planting hadn't started till the Nineties, and this bit we were walking through still had an edgelands quality. 'When you see the evidence of fires that does have a very urban feel,' said Paul.

'It's obviously a young woodland,' he went on:

you can tell by how much grass there still is under the trees.
I'd suspect it was still quite scrubby until about fifteen
years ago. Ivy would have been the first stage, and then if it
was an ancient woodland you'd have bluebells and things,
but now we're talking hundreds of years. The hazels would
have been planted: you've seen those little sprigs planted
alongside motorways in those plastic tubes – that's how that
would have been done. The birches: some would have been
planted, but the rubbly soil, they'd have liked that, and lots
now will have self-seeded.

We headed into what we thought the centre of the wood, Paul tick-
ing off field maple, hazel, holm oak . . .

'Ah: now behind you – this big, blowsy thing that looks like an
apple: I think it could be a quince! And this white stuff' (we'd reached
a clearing, its floor carpeted with white fuzz) 'is poplar – cottonwood.

Not the Grace Gates: the entrance to Wick Woodland's old cricket field from the
River Lea.

The whale's ribcage of boundary planes at Wick Woodland.

I can see why they planted poplars, because we're near a river, but it's still an odd species for a wood. Maybe they wanted to screen out the noise of the motorway.'

We passed four people taking their Staffie for a walk – the only other human beings we'd encountered so far - and then all of a sudden here it was. This path we'd turned along turned out to be made of concrete slabs, now partially covered with soil and leaf mould – and exactly the width of an all-weather cricket wicket.

I stood at the Hackney Wick end while Paul took up his umpiring position at the Homerton Road end: there were wild cherry and hawthorn at mid-on, a cherry laurel over at cover point, and apple trees, already pretty with white blossom, at square leg, and also at gully. 'Now they *will* have been planted,' said Paul: they would have been conspicuously un-natural trees to find in a truly wild wood. 'I suspect when they decided to really make it into a woodland a lot of volunteers will

← Paul Wood cover-driving on the up on the old all-weather wicket.
→ Forest it may be now, but out is still out.

have got involved – lots of people who wanted to plant trees and had an idea of what they wanted, like a fruit tree.' But if you could have fruit trees in the memorial garden of the county ground at Hove, why not here? A bit further back, around where deep fine leg would have been, were two yet more un-native woodland trees: a couple of ornamental cherries frothy with blossom. On and probably beyond the boundary we even found three giant redwoods (though hardly giant yet).

But before any of this wood had grown up, when this concrete wicket base had still been covered with the black composition matting we found flaking off another strip over towards the Homerton Road side – who had charged in to propel the ball down what must have been a good and bouncy track, and who would have carved it away towards where that cherry laurel was and scampered off for a run? Where had these inner-city cricketers come from, and where did they go? And why had it all ceased?

Well, until the mid-Nineties Hackney had a council with no money, had yet to become the destination of choice for the urban gentry priced out of Islington and the artists' communities that colonised the Regent's Canal and London Fields, and the entire site of what is now the Olympic Park was sonorously written off (as always used to infuriate me when the drum was being banged for London's Olympic bid) as 'a vast swathe of dereliction'. Moving into Hackney back then, I liked it just fine, but if sports pavilions kept getting vandalised, say, and youth clubs went short of funding, who could argue for long against turning an under-used or even redundant cricket field into a tranquil, diverse woodland: a solution decades ahead of its time: rewilding?

07

GREEN FIELD PAINTING:

Cricket in Art

W hen we look at a game of cricket, what do we see? When it's not even there in front of us, how do we visualise it?

There are two kinds of cricket art. The first is the photograph in brushstrokes: the kind of respectful, meticulous rendition intended to make you think, 'That's just how he/it looks,' in the same fashion as a great many pictures of steam trains on the Ribblehead Viaduct or Lancasters droning over the Ruhr. When it's a portrait painted to hang in a Long Room or a library it functions more as a statue.

And then there are the figurative artists who try to paint, or can't help painting, what they're *really* seeing: the essence of cricket. Its nature.

They see nature first.

The purest example is Blaise Drummond's 'Untitled Green Field Painting (No. 2)'. Here is the game of cricket abstracted to its essentials: white figures on green – but the green comes first, in its immensity, bleeding off all four edges, with the cricketers, the tiny, scattered, antlike cricketers (the field pushed back, you'd have to say), atomised across it. This is a green world: a natural world: a grass world.

Blaise himself, when we spoke, put his own interest in cricket at 'absolutely minor', though he did commend *Test Match Special* as 'very good for artists working in studios – very serene, people chatting about cream cakes, a good, summery feel . . .' This painting was conceived as one of a series of 'untitled history paintings', along with scenes of planes over London, street trees and 'people lounging in Hyde Park'. But, he went on,

> there's a formal thing about the cream and green of cricket
> that worked well – footballers would have had much
> more strident colours. And one of the attractive things
> about watching sport is that manicured grass – it's very
> artificial, of course: it's actually a faux pastoral. And there's
> an absurdity, a slightly comic pathos, about this kind of

strenuousness, diving and reaching, spread across this petri dish, this flat, green thing. But chasing a ball on a nice summer's day is as good a way to pass our time on the planet as anything . . .

John Heritage is transfixed by the green world of cricket too, but for him it is a geometric artwork in itself: the cricket ground has become the barred lines of the mower's path, and the match itself a kind of *Draughtsman's Contract* masque enclosed within their confining prison.

Go back a century to the Camden House Group, and see how its first president, Spencer Gore, was painting a cricket match in 1909. Influenced by the Post-Impressionists, he saw a game as similarly enclosed by nature – but drenched in flora and foliage: framed and overhung by trees, the female spectator in the foreground apparently ankle-deep in flowers or petals, and the natural world bursting so

← 'Untitled Green Field Painting (No. 2)', Blaise Drummond, 1999.
→ 'The Cricket Match', Spencer Gore, oil on canvas, 1909.

with life that the outfield seems to be not just as tussocky as golf course rough but actually erupting into humps and tumuli as though they're playing on the old *Times* ground at Ravensbourne.

Forward to 1937, and Cecil Lay painting just before the war, with a plane already buzzing ominously overhead. What is the focal point of his 'Cricket Match', with its Stanley Spencerish innocence and hyper-reality? The red-headed youth who has shinned up a tree to secure a vantage-point from which to view the Test match.

When artists aren't painting grass in order to paint cricket, they're painting trees. In 2003 Nigel Purchase painted 'Cricket Match': this time a slightly Lowry-ish tableau, whose foregrounded subject is a teeming party — so many people that it is spilling over onto the path, and everyone oddly oblivious of the action on the field behind them. But what makes the fish-eye-lens perspective of the painting possible, with the wider, deeper circle of the cricket ground enclosing the smaller, nearer gathering? The trees, all arrayed like a stage set. The trees are the gatekeepers to the cricket: the portal. The only way is through them. All this can only take place within the natural world.

These green elements come together in the work of the distinguished modern artist David Inshaw, most famous for his mysterious, spellbinding 'The Badminton Game', which is in the Tate. But his reputation and popularity rest not insignificantly on his cricket paintings.

'Cricket Match', Cecil Lay, 1937.

In 'The Cricket Game', which he has painted in several iterations, the white-clad cricketers are as integral to the pillowy green hills and plump trees as a flock of sheep. There is no human habitation or construction to be seen – not even a pavilion.

If this scene is abstracted from a particular reality it would be somewhere like Ibberton Cricket Club, near Blandford Forum in Dorset – Inshaw himself is based not so far away in Devizes, and subsequently was much inspired in his art by Dorset's Jurassic Coast around West Bay. Ibberton is an actual landscape, with an actual cricket ground buried in it, and hardly a human dwelling to interrupt the glow of green. These places do exist.

'The Cricket Game', David Inshaw, 1976.

What I take from the painting is its timelessness: this golden light never seems destined to fade into dusk; the shadows will lengthen for ever. Cricket here is a long game: as long as the whole summer. You can't write such works off as merely 'pastoral': this is not a bland vision of Arcadia – it stands in the tradition of Paul Nash, even William Blake, whom Inshaw's biographer quotes as opining that 'No Man of Sense ever supposes that copying from Nature is the Art of Painting.' Cricket here is a mysterious ritual: there is something secret and strange about it, like the glow-worms on Egdon Heath in Thomas Hardy's *The Return of the Native*.

Golden light also predominates in one last work of art: a window. And this time the authors, plural, were not the artist but the patrons. When the historical biographer Antonia Fraser and the playwright Harold Pinter married, their wedding present to each other, they decided, would be a stained-glass window. It would depict their favourite things.

Ibberton CC in Dorset: human habitation barely interrupts the green canvas.

Pinter's choice was entirely predictable, perhaps, for a lifelong cricket aficionado who played for the wandering Gaieties side and wrote a wonderful essay, 'Arthur Wellard', about his septuagenarian team-mate, the former Somerset all-rounder who had faced Larwood and bowled against Hammond in a 50-year career. He also, Antonia writes in *Must You Go?*, her memoir of her life with him, 'loved anything that could be construed as "England" – which was perhaps why cricket appealed to him aesthetically so much, the cricket on the village green, the cricket match of a David Inshaw painting . . .' Pinter therefore chose his four favourite cricketers from the game's golden age for the window: Hirst, Spooner, Foster and Briggs – who had also obliviously given their names to the four protagonists of his 1974 play *No Man's Land*.

Antonia Fraser chose her favourite flowers: camellias, roses, honeysuckle . . . Pinter was allowed to add his favourite, the hollyhock. The following year the distinguished stained glass artist Jane Gray had completed the window, datelined with the wedding day itself, 27 November 1980, and ever since it has hung in the London house they shared and where Lady Antonia has continued to live since Pinter's death in 2008.

'It's always been known as the Cricket Window', she told me when I went round to see it. 'Cricket tends to take over everything . . .' Not that she minded in the least: 'I love cricket'. Lady Antonia handed me

'The Cricket Window', Jane Gray, 1981.

a poem she'd written the previous year, 'inspired by Stuart Broad', called 'Harold and Cricket', the first verse of which went:

'It's my passion in life –'
And he didn't mean me.
'Just like a wife –'
And he didn't mean me.

Her father, Lord Longford, had been an eager schoolboy cricketer to the extent that 'he knew *Wisden* off by heart,' and she and her sister, now the novelist Rachel Billington, were taken to watch plenty of cricket matches during their childhood at their father's club, Hurst Green, near Battle in Sussex – 'a lovely ground'. Pyewell Park in Surrey was another of her favourites, presumably visited on the Gaieties' travels – as was the amazing inner-city oasis of the Honourable Artillery Ground at Moorgate in the City of London. 'I'd have loved L. S. Lowry to have done a painting there.'

The Cricket Window was in a room just off the hall, looking out onto the street – 'Taxi drivers often remark on it.' Once again, consecrated in stained glass this time, here was the union of cricket and the natural world. It was a slightly dank day – certainly no sunlight flooding through – but I realised as I took the window in that a single hue unified the cricketing and the natural elements: the gold of the stumps, the bats, the orange tip and brimstone butterflies, the leaves and buds of the trailing flowers, the wife's and the husband's initials, the medallions bearing the cricketers' names.

This game of cricket, I asked Lady Antonia – why did she love it?

'It's about being part of nature in a wonderfully ordered way,' she pondered. 'I don't think there's such a thing as an ugly cricket ground – which is sort of natural . . .'

08

MAMMALS

When it comes to reintroductions of formerly extinct species cricket has been remarkably adventurous. There are now eagles in Essex, sharks in Brighton and, would you believe, bears in Birmingham. Of course, there are Bears in Bristol too these days, and Tigers in Leicester and, I think you'll find, even in Castleford – all playing rugby of one code or another. Still want to bother with beavers in Dorset?

This is the very first time I have ever gone in search of information about the T20! Vitality! Blast!, and I was pleasantly surprised to discover that getting on for half the counties haven't given themselves a slogfest nickname. Middlesex may compete in shirts that make you look like a strawberry Nesquik, but at least they're still just Middlesex. It's a pity too that Sussex have opted for a T20 moniker that would clear the beach at Hove very quickly, when its club crest already features more appropriate and traditional wildlife: the Sussex martlet.

We are pre-empting the next chapter, but let's dwell on the question of adopting an animal of appropriate character for your team to live up to. In what sense can Warwickshire's T20 side really aspire to be bearish? Sore-headed? As gloomy as a falling stock market? The martlet, on the other hand, is a heraldic emblem of avian character that has adorned the actual Sussex county coat of arms since the seventeenth century, though the exact species is arguable. As a mythical beast it is continuously on the wing, apparently (to the extent of lacking feet altogether) – which would suggest the swift. But the six that appear on the county's and cricket club's crests (red and gold in the former, blue and gold in the latter) look more like house martins – while in Germany the martlet is elided into a lark, and in France all the way into a duckling. And as for what the martlet stands for in heraldry, it reminds me of my favourite passage in John Barclay's *The Appeal of the Championship*, a lovely, funny book about Sussex's attempt to win the County Championship in 1981 for the very first time.

It is the second match of Sussex's cricket week at Eastbourne – the county only visit the delightful Saffrons ground these days for the

occasional one-dayer – and a combination of a pitch that 'proved to be as good-natured as it looked' and the ironclad defence of Derbyshire's David Steele and Alan Hill has by mid-afternoon on the final day apparently condemned the match to peter out in a draw. But soon after Hill is run out, Imran Khan, who has been

'Continuous effort': the motto of the county martlets on Imran Khan's chest.

fielding in the deep at square leg and getting mighty bored beneath the giant Town Hall clock, which boomed out its chimes every quarter of an hour, came running over to me with an excited look in his eye.

'Johnny, I want to bowl,' he said.

'You what?' I replied, taken aback.

'Yes, I want to bowl,' Imran insisted. 'Conditions are just right. I am going to put on my bowling boots.' . . .

It was a rare and wonderful thing when your fast bowler actually wanted to bowl and, irrespective of conditions, it was not an opportunity to be turned down lightly . . .

'Give me the ball,' he said, grabbing it and rubbing it gleefully in his hands. He had the remarkable ability to make the oldest and shabbiest ball shine like a pearl. 'Perfect', he said as he marked out his run, and between us we set the field. 'Start defensive,' he said, 'and then, when I am ready, we attack.' I wisely did what I was told, and out of the blue the game came alive.

Dismissing his captain's worries that the old ball 'looks as though it's been chewed by a dog' with the imperious reproof that 'You still do not understand the finer points of fast bowling,' Imran gets it reverse-swinging (though back then no-one knew anything about such an art), immediately traps John Steele LBW and then,

a man inspired, wiped out the rest of the batting. Four wickets in five balls, all bowled or LBW . . .

'That was clever bowling,' he said as he left the field. 'Now I want to bat.'

'Oh, that's good,' I said.

'I want to bat high in the order. I feel it is my day and we must now beat this lot. I shall bat at four,' he said. 'The others won't mind.' . . .

'Why do you always let him have his own way?' someone asked me.

'Because he says he's going to win the match for us.' . . .

Imran, as ever adorned with his floppy hat, entered the stage and began to set about Derbyshire's bowling. He batted like a man on a mission, hit three sixes and eleven fours and laid waste to all that Derbyshire set before him. His hundred that afternoon was one of the county's greatest innings.

A record crowd – 25,000 people came to Eastbourne that week – was ecstatic. It was thrilling stuff. Imran swept Derbyshire aside, and Sussex won in spectacular style with five balls to spare.

Uncapped players for Sussex are allowed just a solitary martlet on their sweater: not until they're awarded their county cap may they sport all six (a complete over, I suppose). It stands – the heraldic martlet – for 'continuous effort'.

When it comes to real animals gracing a cricket field, the native species are, sadly, not usually appreciative of the game. Moles push up molehills on the outfield: not conducive to the passage of a silky cover drive to the boundary. Badgers dig up the outfield even more. In the Forest of Dean wild boar make a right mess of a cricket pitch.

In 2013 a spate of badger attacks – mysteriously prevalent at cricket clubs in the Chilterns – prompted Andy Bull to devote his Spin column in the *Guardian* to a droll investigation of the phenomenon. Certainly the destruction can be prodigious, whether the culprit be badger, boar or indeed crows, and prompt cricket club officials to reach for the military metaphors. 'My first comment was,' Rickmansworth CC's chairman told Andy, '"This looks like something you'd see in the First World War."' 'The ground is like a war-zone,' a

trustee of the 135-year-old Forest CC informed *The Forest Review* in 2015 after wild boar had wrecked the playing surface. Two years later the ground's gates had suspiciously been left open to enable them to root it all up again: 'Nothing has stopped play for this club before. We were going all the way through the war, but we just can't cope with this.'

Andy Bull wondered if the badgers' efforts were in retaliation against the threat of a TB cull – but what do you do to counter the ravages of a protected species? His research on possible deterrents threw up everything from male human urine (a bottled product called Slash Away that Rickmansworth's groundsman flatly refused to water his precious greensward with) to lion dung. Alternatively, you could badger-proof your cricket ground by erecting electric fencing round the boundary – which 'would have the corollary benefit of saving on laundry costs by deterring fielders from diving around the outfield'. Rickmansworth went for garlic spray, at a cost of hundreds of pounds. 'They were, at least, now secure against vampire attack,' records Bull. 'But the badgers were entirely undeterred.'

If it's crows that are actually doing all the digging, apparently you need an 'air cannon, which will detonate 125-decibel thunderclaps

← Wild boar did this: Yorkley Star CC's Alex Kear surveys the war-zone.
→ Badgers did this at Rickmansworth.

across your ground every five minutes or so'. 'It strikes me,' Andy Bull came to conclude,

> that the expert advice, which is to surround your pitch with electric fences, smother it in dung and urine, festoon it with scarecrows and set up an air cannon to blaze away overhead, is going to make your ground feel a lot more like the Somme than anything the badgers were ever going to do to it.

Though domesticated rather than feral, a more discerning beast from the late-nineteenth century, long before groundsmen had tractors and Blotters and Brumbrellas, was celebrated by J. L. Carr in *Carr's Dictionary of Extra-Ordinary Cricketers*: Horace, 'a horse of such exquisite sensibility that, when Fred Morley, the invariable Notts last man, left the Trent Bridge Pavilion, it sidled unobtrusively towards the roller.'

Leicestershire CCC's nickname, the Foxes, derives from a properly local emblem – the Quorn Hunt has long been one of the most well-known in the country. There is a fox on the club crest, and a rather smart gold one on the bespoke-tailored green jacket the club captain wears out to the middle for the toss. But nowadays foxes are largely a metropolitan phenomenon. According to the BBC's *Winterwatch*, I gather, evolution has already seen the urban fox develop a slightly narrower jaw: its mandibles are no longer needed to crack open a freshly killed rabbit's ribcage, but only to masticate a half-eaten Whopper.

The best chance of seeing one is at the Oval. There, a rather sad juvenile specimen interrupted a game between Surrey and Glamorgan in 2019 to relieve itself on the square in front of (the tabloids noted with satisfaction) 24,500 spectators. Glamorgan, who were fielding at the time, lived down to the fox's verdict by then getting bowled out for 44, the lowest total in T20 history. It would be tempting to credit the

fox with admirable judgement when it comes to the white-ball game, were it not that, during the 2020 Bob Willis Trophy, in an echoing stadium, another resident mooched proprietorially out to the middle during the luncheon interval for a repeat performance.

I've often thought the campaign to bring back fox hunting misdirected: there aren't any foxes in the countryside any more for the green Barbour brigade to hunt. You need to legalise it in *Lambeth*. Then we'd have some sport, watching the Old Kent Road Hunt thunder off to the 'Post Horn Gallop' a-whooping and ululating round the Elephant and Castle gyratory and get a ticket stopping in a bus lane for the kill.

Next we come to the category of what we might call indigenous incursors. Depending on the location of the cricket ground, the game can be interrupted by various species. At Teddington Town CC in West London's Bushy Park red and fallow deer frequently stray onto the

An Oval fox, sadly uninterested in the proceedings out in the middle.

↑ Deer share Bushy Park with Teddington Town CC's cricketers.
↓ New Forest ponies calmly graze the outfield at Lyndhurst CC.

outfield. In the New Forest a number of grounds are grazed by New Forest ponies, while Graham Standring of the Yorkshire Wildlife Trust used to play for Tavistock in Devon, where the cricket ground was 'right on the edge of an open area of Dartmoor. I had to clear up after the Dartmoor ponies before each game,' he reflects, 'and once had to delay a match whilst a pony gave birth on the outfield!' And in 2002 *Wisden*'s Index of Unusual Occurrences noted with delightful vagueness that in Finland 'a while back, play was stopped when an elk galloped out of the woods.'

In late 1989 the *Times* sportswriter Simon Barnes followed the England team out to Delhi for a one-off tournament to celebrate the centenary of Jawarlhal Nehru's birth. 'Getting fed up with watching the guys practise,' he recalls, 'I was prowling round the perimeter . . . and I found a mongoose.' When England were touring India in 2012/13 and playing a warm-up match at Motera (since rebuilt as the Narendra Modi Stadium in Ahmedabad), there was a monkey. In Sri Lanka, during England's winter 2020 Test series, it was monitor lizards (OK, reptiles, not mammals) – the TV cameras picking up a particular specimen venturing in front of a perimeter advertising board.

And then we come to the non-native incursors: what we'd have to call invasive species, if they actually took up residence, but that aren't strictly speaking wildlife – just too good to ignore. The 24th of November 2011 became the first and so far only instance of a zebra at Lord's, in the company of the then England captain Andrew Strauss, to unveil the Test team's new sponsor, the South African bank Investec, which insisted on a literal embodiment of its logo. The surprisingly large animal, which looks large enough for Strauss to have won a Gold Cup on, 'made it closer to the pavilion than most men in history have', notes Abishek Mukherjee on the excellent CricketCountry website, ruefully.

In 2007 Stephen Lovell, landscapist and garden designer by profession, 'mini-naturalist' by preference, answered an advertisement

↑ Motera, India, 2012: even monkeys shouldn't walk in front of the sightscreen.
↓ Lord's 2011. No jacket means the zebra's barred from the pavilion.

Payagala cricket ground in Sri Lanka after the tsunami:
↑ restoring the wicket; ↓ the elephant blessing the pitch.

for help with a 'post-tsunami project in Sri Lanka'. It turned out to be the restoration of a cricket pitch wrecked by the floods in Payagala, for a *Challenge Anneka* programme on ITV. Stephen's team had frequently to contend with little land monitors scuttling across the pitch while they were trying to repair it, he recalls, but when it came time to hand it back to the cricket club there was much 'life-affirming' festivity. The great Aravinda da Silva was the guest of honour – Stephen even got to bat with him against the club's under-14s in the first match – with 'lots of people blessing the pitch'. Then came the real guest of honour, attired in a large robe, with its *mahout*: the ceremonial elephant - which proceeded to plod straight across the newly restored pitch . . .

But an elephant had a part to play on an even more historic day in cricket history, and once again it was at the Oval. I commend Arunabha Sengupta's 'The day India ended England's home rule', on the CricketCountry website, on which I have drawn.

India had never won a Test series – or even a single Test – in England, but on 24 August 1971 they found themselves coming into the third and final Test of the series all square, with the first two drawn. England under Ray Illingworth gained a first innings lead of 71, but the fourth day was to turn the game. Brian Luckhurst and John Jameson had put on 23 for the first wicket, but then the Indian leg-spinner Chandrasekhar struck, and by lunch England were already three down, with Jameson, Edrich and Fletcher already back in the pavilion.

And then, during the luncheon interval, came the elephant. This fourth day of the Test fell on the start of Ganesha Chaturthi, the Hindu festival celebrating the birth of the elephant-headed deity Ganesh, the god of prosperity and wisdom, so members of the local Indian community had hired Bella the elephant from Chessington Zoo (as it was then: not yet a World of Adventures) to plod around the outfield.

Bella's perambulation (as it would certainly have been announced at Lord's) cannot but have been propitious. Chandreskhar finished with six wickets and India needed only 173 to win. Though Sunil

Gavaskar went for nought to John Snow that evening they got the runs on the final day with four wickets to spare, with Abid Ali square -cutting the winning ball for four, though jubilant Indian supporters scooped it up well before it reached the boundary. 'India was a colony of England,' the Indian wicket-keeper Farokh Engineer subsequently explained to *The Times*, 'and to beat your masters at their own game was a bit of a feather in the cap.'

Bella the elephant's perambulation of the Oval during Ganesh Chaturthi, Third Test, 1971.

09

BIRDS

W hy is there a common crossover between birdwatchers and cricket fans? Discuss.

For starters, the two activities share the same requirement for forensic attention: is that a black-tailed or a bar-tailed godwit, and what distinguishing features enable you to decide? Is that the googly coming out of the leg-spinner's hand or the flipper, or just the one that goes on with the arm – and *how do you tell*? These things matter. As a watcher, you need binoculars for both.

There is also the same pleasure in cataloguing, categorisation and classification: in recording the exact outcome of every ball in a score-book; of working out bowling figures at the end of a day's play; of the finality of the scorecard at the close (at Lord's the true spectator will purchase one to fill in before play starts, and queue up again when it's over for a second, printed record of the day's progress. I regret this is no longer letterpress, as it was in my day.) And a comparable satisfaction – necessity - in tallying up all the sightings of a day's birding: 2 great tit; grey heron; 50 goldfinch; c.100 wigeon; marsh harrier (juv. fem.) . . . My friend Stephen still does, into a Dictaphone, and he'd take the trouble to get them in the correct taxonomic order too. It is about wild hazard and contingency reduced, or at least frozen, in order and neatness. We now *know what happened*.

If we're talking about serious birding, then it's also the case that these are both competitive sports. Just as you are compiling your tally of runs or wickets during each season, and watching your average, so the birder has his year list, his life list, and his local patch list (your local patch is the one nearby location you designate as the one you will watch regularly, all year round, to the point of familiarity; your home ground, in cricket terms). The statistical aspect is crucial, in the race against others and yourself: the figures cannot lie. Every new species is a contribution, just as much as each four or LBW. Can you beat what you did last year?

And I guess that, apart from golf, cricket is the only sport in which habitat is as important as it is in birdwatching. Avocets will gravitate to salt marsh as readily as Richard Hadlee did to the greentop Notts had back then at Trent Bridge. England got trounced in the Third Test at Ahmedabad in 2021 picking a bowling attack for a seamers' wicket and finding a turner from day one. A windy day will see birds hunker down in the bushes out of sight; a humid one will raise hopes of the ball swinging. None of these considerations affects the outcome of games at Anfield or the Emirates. Proper cricket fans will go to watch county cricket at Scarborough, or Arundel, or Tunbridge Wells, or indeed Lord's, regardless of who they support, because they're just beautiful places for this game to be played. (Why does the ECB never get this, and make it a positive, priceless marketing asset? Why no county cricket festival at Sidmouth's beachside ground, to create a Scarborough Festival of the South-West?)

All this is also why birders and cricket fans are overwhelmingly male.

Like the bird life of your local patch, the bird life of cricket grounds can be divided in two. There are the indigenous, expected species, and then there are the one-offs, the migrants and strays, the irruptions.

The expected species, however, can change. You would expect to see, as you do, herring gulls dotting the outfield at North Marine Road ground in Scarborough: the pealing clamour of gulls, as Bill Oddie has noted, always used to be how you knew you'd arrived at the seaside.

Herring gull discovering that a bail is much less digestible than a chip.

Some years ago the cricket writer Gideon Haigh, browsing in a sec-
ondhand bookshop in Hove, came across a copy of the legendarily
cantankerous Rowland Bowen's *Cricket: A History*, an esoteric but
astounding work. 'No sooner had I taken possession than a seagull
dropped a huge crap on the cover,' he recalled. 'I took this as a good
omen.'

But now there are gulls in our cities almost as plentiful as the
urban pigeons. In recent decades years herring gulls and lesser black-
backed gulls have moved inland in big numbers: a lot less fish in the
sea thanks to overfishing has been offset by a lot more fast food and
eating on the move. Today's herring gull is more likely to subsist on
fish and chips or discarded Filet-o-Fish burgers than on herrings, and
gets as plump on them as we do. The distinguished birder and author
of *The Red Kite's Year* Ian Carter notes how the lesser black-backed
and herring gulls 'come alive' during the T20 games he frequently
attends at Taunton,

> swirling around the ground and diving down to pick up
> any discarded or unfinished bits of food they can find. The
> evening games are great for this with the floodlights, and lots
> of hungry, alcohol-fuelled spectators eating lots of food and
> not necessarily finishing it all in the short break between
> innings. It's quite a sight.

But gulls and limited-overs cricket go back long before it became
'the white-ball game'. The great John Arlott, whose only television
commentaries were for the BBC's John Player Sunday League 40-over
matches, a somewhat formulaic format even then, once apparently
observed: 'Before we began there was a flock of crows down in front
of the far stand. They've been replaced by seagulls. I assume the crows
won the toss and elected to bat.'

Gulls may have migrated inland from the seaside, but waterfowl

you wouldn't generally expect to see at a cricket ground. Except Worcester. During the winter months the low-lying county ground is regularly submerged (like the nearby racecourse and much of the rest of the town) when prolonged rain causes the River Severn to burst its banks. Not infrequently do Worcestershire's early home matches of the county season have to be transferred to Kidderminster while the playing surface dries out. Which is why mallard are on the list here for the cricket naturalist.

Back during the First World War, when first-class cricket was suspended, you'd have found geese at Lord's – hardly rare, but certainly indigenous, as the ground was used as a goose farm. Go to watch Middlesex these days on their excursions to outgrounds while Lord's is used for Test matches, and you'll almost be guaranteed of seeing red kites. Extinct in England since 1871, they were reintroduced from 1990 in the Chilterns, when two young birds from the surviving breeding colony in mid-Wales and 11 flown over from Spain were released, with John Paul Getty's Wormsley estate, that includes the idyllic cricket

← A mallard at a flooded New Road, Worcester.
→ Lord's used as a goose farm during the First World War, 1915.

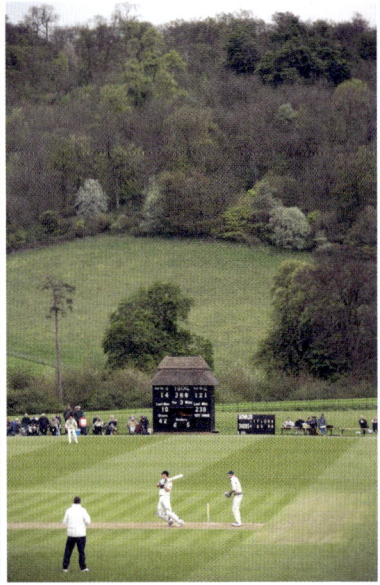

ground he built with its thatched pavilion, one of the reintroduction sites. For the first few years the kites' roost was right alongside the cricket field. Since the introductions the species, a carrion scavenger, has successfully spread to 200 pairs in the Chilterns alone. 'Always thought the red kites that flew over Wormsley as I came out to bat were being a bit harsh,' reflects Ian Marshall, editor of the *Playfair Cricket Annual*. I wonder how long it will be before they start swooping down at T20 matches along with the gulls to hoover up unwanted junk food.

A harbinger of the red kites' steadily increasing range, effectively following the M25 both clockwise and anti-clockwise, was the individual spotted by Stephen Moss in 2006 from a hospitality box at Lord's when he was meant to be watching England playing Sri Lanka. Now you can see red kites over Reading town centre, and as far east as Stevenage

Red kites were re-introduced from 1990 in the Chilterns, including on the Wormsley Estate where John Paul Getty built his bucolic cricket ground.

to the north and Rainham Marshes all the way along the Thames near the Dartford Bridge, and you can certainly see them when Middlesex play at the improbably vast playing fields of Merchant Taylors' School in Northwood, wheeling and mewing above the avenue of red horse chestnut trees. Other reintroduction programmes have included 68 released from 1999 in Yorkshire at Harewood House near Leeds, which is why one was spied wafting across the sightscreen at Headingley during an England-New Zealand Test.

On the other hand, some familiar inhabitants suddenly disappear. 'When I started playing cricket at Chardstock in East Devon', writes Rob Blackwell, 'summer cricket was often accompanied by the song of the skylark. With the change from hay to silage and the earlier cutting this wonderful birdsong disappeared.' For those of us who grew up in suburbia during the Sixties the house sparrow was a ubiquitous bird, in gardens, in parks, everywhere, and it certainly would have been at Lord's back in 1936 when one was hit and killed by a ball struck by Jehangir Khan while MCC were playing Cambridge University. Over recent years, however, house sparrow numbers have plunged, with mooted causes ranging from the pollution from internal combustion engines to the destruction of hedges in suburban gardens to make

way for block paving and high fences, to the incessant hubbub of city traffic confusing their mating calls. Whatever the diagnosis, the Lord's sparrow is now, along with Denis Compton's kneecap, probably the prize exhibit at the Lord's Museum, not least because these days seeing a house sparrow in London – even one stuffed,

The Lord's sparrow, hit and killed by a ball in 1936.

stapled to the fatal ball and stuck on a plinth – is quite a notable event.

Abroad, of course, the indigenous species are simply different. At the Test ground in Colombo in Sri Lanka it's not pigeons that settle on the square but egrets; in South Africa, sacred ibis. Simon Barnes saw a shikra – a small bird of prey also known as the little banded goshawk - at the Wankhede cricket stadium in Mumbai. In 1960 Alan Ross was covering the MCC tour of the West Indies (as England's overseas forays were then officially titled). Reporting on the Second Test in Port of Spain in Trinidad, a notorious occasion at which the crowd at Queen's Park Oval rioted after the home team's Charan Singh had been adjudged run out, Ross, staying 'in my air-conditioned cell at the Queen's Park Hotel … would try and write, to the ceaseless questionings of the yellow-breasted, badger-crested *Qu'est ce qui dit* birds that flashed through the flamboyant and monkey pots beneath my window'. And the pigeons at the ground, 'on their endless, undeterred circuits', were white: probably rock doves or white-tipped doves.

Ross's subsequent book about the tour, *Through the Caribbean*, is magnificently sensuous and colourful: a true, and distinguished, work of travel writing as much as a sports book, every bit as alive to the natural world as to the cricket that was played. People don't write cricket books like this nowadays, more's the pity. We'll return to it in the chapter on 'The Cricket Naturalist in Literature'.

A quarter-century later, Simon Barnes was in the Caribbean for another England tour, and watching the Test at Port of Spain once more. It was the 1986 series, the West Indies' fearsome all-pace attack, on this occasion Holding, Marshall, Garner and the debutant Patrick Patterson, was in its pomp, and the First Test, at Sabina Park in Kingston, Jamaica, played with low sightscreens on a corrugated pitch, with Patterson sending down bouncers at 100mph, is remembered as 'the scariest Test ever played', 'cricket's equivalent of the Somme', and the only match where even the great Graham Gooch confessed to having felt unsafe. 'It was the first time in history,' wrote Rob Smyth

In England we get pigeons and gulls on the outfield: ↑ in South Africa it's sacred ibis; ↓ in Sri Lanka it's cattle egret (here on the covers at rainy Colombo).

in a superb retrospective feature in the *Guardian*, 'a team went 5-0 down after one Test.' By the time the caravan had moved on to Trinidad it was the visitors who were in rebellious mood.

'I was writing a biography of Phil Edmonds,' recalls Simon Barnes,

and I'd been flown out by the publisher. I was staying up in the hills in a lodging-house, and had my bins, and I'd brought a book on *The Birds of Trinidad and Tobago* by a guy called ffrench.

There'd been a local match and then a Test match, and the tour was falling to pieces before my eyes — they'd had a terrible time at Sabina Park, and Phil Edmonds was wearing a bruise like a black corset which he used to show off in the swimming pool. It had to be somebody's fault, this whole dreadful thing.

Port of Spain Oval, Trinidad: by the Second Test here in 1986 England were already 5-0 down.

In Port of Spain England were quickly in trouble again, dismissed in their first innings for just 176, with Ian Botham making just 2. He'd be dismissed for a single in the second innings, and it would be another heavy defeat, this time by 7 wickets.

> Botham went out to bat, came back, having been dismissed
> cheaply, and made a noose gesture at the press box – 'Go on,
> guys, hang me'. At which point the TV cameraman swung
> round to show half a dozen guys all staring mutely back …
> Except one, and that was me, looking the other way, because
> I'd just seen a crested oropendola. It was a lovely bird – it
> was on the cover of the ffrench book – and oropendolas built
> these wonderful hanging nests …

A lovely bird indeed, with its long lemon-yellow tail, and that crest so hair-slender as to be scarcely visible.

But while crested oropendolas are the kind of bird you might hope to see at Port of Spain (if you weren't straining to pick up Patrick Patterson's chin-music), there are also the birds you wouldn't expect. Simon Barnes once saw a peregrine at Lord's from the Media Centre (over the Nursery pitch, again looking away from where the action was supposed to be), and then there was his club cricket for his village team in Hertfordshire:

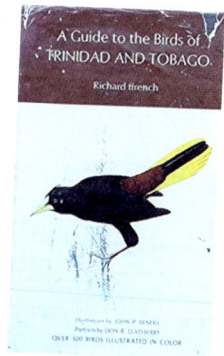

> When I was playing for Tewin Irregulars, on
> at least one occasion we played the RSPB, and
> I remember once stopping the bowler in his
> delivery stride to point out a cuckoo flying

A crested oropendola on the cover of Richard ffrench's field guide: Simon Barnes should have been watching Botham.

overhead. Any other team, there would have been severe retribution, but he pulled back and said, 'Good spot!' and went back to his mark.

The black stork is, according to *Birds of London*, a 'rare vagrant', and the only sighting at all it records in central London in the twentieth century is from 25 August 1990, when one was seen 'drifting over the Oval in Kennington while England were playing a Test match'. With the match drawn after India scored 606/9 in their first innings this may have been the highlight for anyone who spied it.

For some reason hoopoes, more regular summer visitors but still a very good spot, seem especially attracted to cricket grounds: a recent example saw the long lenses deployed at Collingham Cricket Club in North Yorkshire as it quietly probed the square for beetles and larvae. Penzance Cricket Club has hosted another, and Edwinstowe, on the doorstep of Sherwood Forest, a third.

The most outlandish vagrant record for a cricket ground has to be from Jeremy Pound: 'In the 2008 test versus South Africa at Edgbaston,' he claims, 'I saw a cassowary running across the outfield' – before rather spoiling it by adding, 'Admittedly, I'd had a beer or two.' Unquestionably corroborated, however, and for birders equally sensational, is the experience of the late Derek Moore. Moore would go on to a distinguished career in nature conservation, helping to build the famous Scrape at Minsmere, becoming director of the Suffolk Wildlife Trust and then chief executive of the Wildlife Trust of South and West Wales, as well as having shared the stage with the Kinks and the Who during his blues band days. He was also a club cricketer in Suffolk of somewhat Bothamesque deportment, and towards the end of the 1965 season - 5 September, to be precise - was due to be playing a match at the Denes Oval ground in Lowestoft.

That morning Moore got up and opened the curtains. 'To my amazement,' he relates in his autobiography *Birds: Coping with an*

Obsession, 'there was a pied fly-catcher on our clothes line, and then another and another.' Out in the garden he counted no fewer than 17 more. 'This was very unusual', he adds unnecessarily. At lunch time he went down to the chippie (none of your salad lunches for cricketers in those days) 'and noted whinchats and common redstarts everywhere. They were not just in the typical habitat but also in the gutters and even in the middle of the road.'

What had happened was a unique collision of circumstances. Light rain that night off the East Anglian coast had coincided with a huge passage of passerines migrating south from Scandinavia. Temporarily disoriented by the rain, the migrants sought landfall down a narrow belt of the coast from Lowestoft to Ipswich, in what would come to be mythicised in birding legend as 'the Great Fall'.

As soon as Moore arrived at the cricket ground in Lowestoft after lunch the groundsman called him over. 'He described how, when he

The tiny speck holding the attention of all the long lenses at Collingham CC is a rare hoopoe.

was cutting the wicket in the late morning, he saw what he thought was smoke coming onto the ground from the beach area.' To his amazement they turned out to be birds, exhausted and dying, dropping out of the sky onto the cricket pitch. Knowing Moore's interest, he had gathered up those he could and put the dead ones in a cardboard box and the survivors to warm by his boiler. 'Imagine the joy of taking dozens of Common Redstarts, Whinchats, Pied Flycatchers and other less common species and warming them in my hands,' writes Moore, 'before releasing them into the shrubbery behind the pavilion.' But the best was to come.

> When the match started we were fielding first and I
> concocted a tale for the captain, saying that I was feeling a
> bit queasy and could I field on the boundary instead of at
> my usual second slip. This achieved, I spent two hours on
> the fringe of the field with Wrynecks, an Ortolan Bunting,
> Bluethroat and many commoner species, while pretending
> to note what was happening in the middle. I cannot
> remember anything about the cricket on that day but I will
> never forget what a spectacle I had just witnessed.

Denes Oval, Lowestoft, 5 September 1965: a landfall of fabulously rare vagrants on the outfield including ← bluethroat and → ortolan bunting.

10

BUTTERFLIES, MOTHS AND INSECTS

'Britain's moths decline by a third in 50 years, study finds,' ran the headline in the *Guardian* to a piece by Patrick Barkham on 3 March 2020. In southern Britain the fall in numbers was even worse – almost 40% – with the stout dart down over 80% in ten years. The major driver for such declines, as you'd expect, is the usual suspect: habitat loss, thanks largely to modern agribusiness and the sterile, monocultural prairies created by its chemical warfare on pests.

The melancholy truth is that as the years go by there is just a lot less wildlife around in Britain. A *lot* less. In *Cricket Country*, the dreamy schoolboy in the halcyon matches of Edmund Blunden's Edwardian childhood in Kent, dismissed early on, wanders off, 'the circuit of the field which falls away to the stream … wide enough for him to be still strolling away and watching the blue moths among the sorrel when the downfall of his team mates arrives'. These blue moths wouldn't have been 'a sighting': they were just part of the scenery. Even when Brian Close was still careering round the roads of Britain at RAC Rally speeds, knees gripping the wheel as he leafed through the *Sporting Life*, I'm sure night drives from a late-finishing Benson & Hedges Cup tie in Taunton to the following morning's County Championship match at Dover would have seen the windscreen splattered with smashed bugs. It is likely that this 2005 correspondent to the *Daily Telegraph* would find it harder today to offer his ingenious tip:

> SIR – Readers wishing to improve their hand-eye
> co-ordination should try catching flies in flight with one
> hand. When I played cricket I found this beneficial for
> fielding at first slip.
>
> G. A. Baxter
> Walton

If laying habitat loss at cricket's door seems extreme, the butterfly

expert and cricket enthusiast Matthew Oates recalls 'Clouded Yellows patrolling the outfield of the county grounds at Taunton and old
Northlands Road, Southampton, including the scarce pale female
form helice.' I wonder if they're still there since Northlands Road
was turned into a housing estate of cul-de-sacs like Greenidge Close?
Fortunately the old Southampton ground's successor turns out to be
fruitful too for the lepidopterist: the magnificent butterfly of which
Matthew has made a particular study, Purple Emperor, 'is breeding just outside the Rose Bowl – Ben Stokes could hit a six into the
breeding sallows.' Matthew has also recorded a 'big White-letter
Hairstreak colony on the elm next to the third man boundary' of the
cricket ground of his old school, Christ's Hospital in Sussex (which, he
notes, 'produced J. A. Snow'), plus a Queen of Spain Fritillary caught
there in 1945.

'But the real issue', Matthew is at pains to stress,

Butterflies at the cricket: ← Clouded Yellow (Northlands Road); →↑ Purple Emperor
(Rose Bowl); →↓ Mountain Ringlet (Cork hat-trick on *TMS*).

is what naturalists do whilst listening to *TMS*. I am at my very happiest whilst out butterflying with *TMS* on my old pocket radio. I can tell you where I was and what I was doing during great moments in the history of *TMS* (e.g. I celebrated Dominic Cork's hat-trick against West Indies on Wrynose Breast in the Lake District High Fells, versus Mountain Ringlet).

Habitat loss need not be as severe as covering a cricket ground with houses to cause a decline in biodiversity, though, as the Essex naturalist and village cricketer Tim Gardiner explains in his paper, 'More runs, fewer crickets'. He means the kind that chirp: 'My passion for the study of crickets (Orthoptera) is equalled by my enthusiasm for the game of cricket.' Crickets and grasshoppers are both members of the order Orthoptera, and both stridulate, or chirp: the difference is that crickets do it by rubbing their wings together, and grasshoppers by rubbing their hind legs *against* their wings. Until the 1950s, when the village cricket grounds of Tim's native Essex were meadows still grazed by sheep or cows,

> We can only imagine how good the grazed outfields, with patches of tall grass, would have been for insects. For example, the insect diversity of grazed pastures can be quite high, with patches of tall vegetation forming a refuge for grasshoppers such as the Meadow Grasshopper, which uses such areas as shelter from avian predation, inclement weather and excessively 'hot' microclimatic temperatures. Butterflies such as Common Blue, Meadow Brown and the Biodiversity Action Plan (BAP) species, Small Heath, would no doubt have been in abundance in the outfield. The latrine areas, where livestock dung was deposited, would also have had tall vegetation due to avoidance of these patches by

grazing animals - these tussocks would have been bustling
with grasshoppers and bush-crickets. Movements of
Meadow Grasshoppers from heavily grazed, short vegetation
to tall grassland habitats in latrine areas have been
noted in a recent study on the Writtle College Estate near
Chelmsford. Movements were highly directional, possibly
instigated by grasshoppers 'seeing' favourable habitat over
short distances . . . It is therefore possible that a basking
grasshopper, disturbed by the passage of the ball through the
sward, would have leapt to the nearest tussock!

But grasshoppers, says Tim, 'are known to suffer mortality during
mechanised mowing of hay meadows in the UK', so the move to gang
mowers to cut cricket fields will have led to far lower numbers, either
through death by mower or loss of habitat, with 'the resultant short,

←↑ Meadow Grasshopper; →↑ Brown Argus at Chignal CC; ←↓ Roesel's Bush
Cricket (common in long grass beyond boundary); →↓ Black-tailed Skimmer.

homogenous sward . . . unsuitable for sustained reproductive or feeding activities'.

Let us join Tim in giving thanks, then, for 'one of my favourite grounds in the county': Matching Green, near Harlow.

> This is a lovely ground, and the surrounds of the
> outfield have very long grass and unimproved grassland
> (unploughed, not sprayed with pesticides), plant species
> such as Heath Bedstraw, Lady's Bedstraw and Sheep's Sorrel.
> The hay meadow also contains an abundance of grasshoppers
> and butterflies such as Common Blue and Small Heath. The
> surrounding ponds are frequented by dragonflies such as
> the Black-tailed Skimmer. These grounds remain a link to
> the cricket fields of the past, which were more than likely as
> important to insects as to leather on willow . . . At Matching
> Green, cricket takes place in harmony with the flora and
> fauna, and the experience of the cricketer is immeasurably
> enhanced by it.

Bee numbers have also plummeted in recent decades, to the extent of prompting real worries as to how our flowers, plants and trees will be pollinated if such a trend continues – the culprit in this case appearing to be the neonicotinoid pesticides the agricultural industry uses to, er, protect its crops. Perhaps consequently, the only official cricket records (i.e. *Wisden*) that involve bees and wasps in any quantity appear to be restricted to Africa: an England A match against Zimbabwe in Harare in 1990, and Namibia's 2003 series against Zimbabwe, at both of which players and umpires were forced to lie flat on the ground to avoid a swarm of bees. However, *Wisden* does (also in its Index of Unusual Occurrences section appended to each volume) judge that 'the most notable event' of a four-day County Championship game between Surrey and Yorkshire at the Oval was 'the arrival of a member of the groundstaff with bucket, spade and besom to deal with some wasps which had congregated at the Vauxhall End'. A similar predicament is recorded with unspecified insects at a one-day game at Arundel in 2004 between Sussex and Yorkshire:

Yorkshire won with 18.1 overs to spare. They did so in dark blue kit, after Wood went out to toss in their intended yellow away shirt and was attacked by a swarm of insects.

The groundstaff were also called into action once at the Home of Cricket itself, as Erica McAllister records in *The Secret Life of Flies*, to deal with a plague of crane fly larvae (daddy-long-legs' babies). *Tipula oleracea*, more commonly called leatherjackets, feed on winter cereal crops, she explains, and especially if the previous crop was oilseed rape. 'These larvae generally live just below the surface of the soil, munching away on the cereal roots. If it's been particularly wet they emerge from the soil, to consume the exposed lower parts of the plant.' Here is the reason, by the way, for those badger and crow assaults on village cricket club outfields: normally half a badger's diet is earthworms, but when earthworms are scarce they go hunting for leatherjacket and cockchafer larvae – and they won't stop pecking and digging till they find them…

But in 1935 several thousand of these leatherjacket larvae had to be removed from the Lord's turf 'and burned, as they caused "bald patches on the wicket", resulting in unpredictable conditions for spin bowlers for most of the remainder of the season.' *Perfect* conditions, Erica.

For nearly 90 years this story has possessed the delicious obscurity guaranteed to relegate it to (and sanctify in) those close-typed pages at the back of a past *Wisden*. But, merely days after I had drafted this chapter, there was a report on the BBC Sport website that Sussex were going to have to switch their first County Championship match of

the 2021 season, against Lancashire, to an away fixture, because Hove had been attacked by an infestation of . . . leatherjackets. It prompted Simon Burnton, in the *Guardian*'s Spin column, to research the 1935 Lord's outbreak.

'Give me a few thrushes and blackbirds, with battalions of starling and sparrows,' he quotes the Lord's groundsman Harry White as fulminating, 'and we would have no leatherjackets at Lord's. But in the summer months the birds prefer to go further afield, and for years now the task of keeping down the leatherjackets has been left to a few sparrows and myself.' Cavalry charging a tank battalion. These 'baby-long-legs, if you will', in Burnton's appellation, consumed not just the wicket but White's long career: Lord's called for the Oval's

---

'Leatherjackets CC take the field': *Winnie-the-Pooh* illustrator E. H. Shephard's *Punch* cartoon of the invasion of Lord's, 1935.

head groundsman, and after 26 years White retired.

It gets worse.

> On the first eight days of play at Lord's that summer
> an astonishing 135 wickets fell, with batsmen happy to
> blame the grubs rather than their own incompetence (the
> situation was so severe that the *Guardian*'s report on the
> Test against South Africa at Lord's that July mentions that
> 'Farrimond stopped a nasty ball from Dalton, rendering
> three leatherjackets unconscious') – and that's not all the
> leatherjackets were blamed for.
>
> Among the staff working at Lord's at the start of that
> summer of 1935 was 18-year-old Ronald Noble of Cautley
> Avenue, Clapham. But in May he was suddenly taken ill,
> and doctors at St James's Hospital in Balham could not save
> him. He died of blood poisoning, but a post-mortem failed
> to establish how it happened. Among the possible reasons
> considered at the inquest into his death was those pesky
> leatherjackets.

Back to moths. Other important causes of the precipitous decline in numbers noted by Patrick Barkham include, as you would imagine, climate change, but also 'possibly, light pollution'. Here, I think we can put cricket in the dock.

It is the Summer Game. Always has been. Played when the sun is out and the days are long and the wickets hard and dry. You start around 11, and you play all the way through the day until the shadows lengthen around 6. If you're watching down at Hove, you can recline in a stripy deckchair at the Cromwell Road end and bask. *That's* cricket.

But nowadays in this country, the first-class game *doesn't play*

cricket on summer days. It starts the County Championship in April, when the weather is grey, showery, windy and cold, and the green pitches are a seamer's paradise – and as soon as we get to June, it stops . . . and doesn't start again until September to finish the Championship off, by which time the mornings are dewy and the days are short and more often than not the players traipse off for bad light around 4. And in between, in July and August – high summer – we wait all the way through the hours of daylight, without playing cricket, until . . . dusk – when we switch on towers of high-wattage floodlights and play a T20 six-hitting firework display until it's pitch dark. (Has Wimbledon thought of moving over to an ace-hitting contest not starting until nightfall? Is Augusta planning to reduce four 18-hole rounds of the Masters to a driving competition down the first to wrap the whole thing up in an evening?)

It's not even as if this array of incandescence capable of laying down a flarepath for an airliner necessarily leads to more hours of

Red sky at night over a floodlit Swalec Stadium in Cardiff portends fine weather – so why not play the cricket during the day?

proper county cricket being reclaimed from bad light: I've sat through hours of daylight watching the floodlights blazing away over an empty pitch . . . while the umpires tucked away in the pavilion decide the 'natural light' is still too poor to play.

Never mind the madness of all this from a cricketing point of view, though I have to admit that I no longer expect to be able to spend the summers of my retirement watching county cricket. I think it will have all gone by then. Let's concentrate on climate change and the light pollution.

How much energy – at least half of it still generated from fossil fuels – is burned entirely unnecessarily by those blazing lights, and contributing to global warming and climate change? And this is something we've only decided to start doing just as it's become clear that our energy use has to diminish quickly if the planet is not to fry. Indeed, in May 2021, commenting on a BBC report on the impact climate change will have on sport, none other than the England cricket captain Joe

Hampshire's atmospheric ground at Northlands Road in Southampton had Clouded Yellows on the outfield. Then it was turned into a housing estate.

Root spoke of how 'It is scary to think the game as it is right now may not be the case in 30 years' time.' He should know, having ended up in hospital on the 2018 Ashes tour after batting at the Sydney Cricket Ground in temperatures of 47.3° (117° Fahrenheit).[1]

But also, how far does this eerie, pearlescent glow bathing the ground displace the natural night? No wonder our towns and cities are never properly dark these days, or that our moth population, largely crepuscular, is on the slide. And all in order to play a crude, synthetic mutation of cricket at the wrong time instead of a day's proper cricket at not just the right time, but the very best time.

---

1 On 25 May 2021 the *Guardian*'s cricket newsletter The Spin published a timely and touching account, 'The Essex village cricket club going in to bat against climate crisis', of the efforts by the Eight Ash Green club to reduce its carbon footprint, from car-sharing to matches to banning plastic in the bar, planting trees and keeping the margins around the playing area 'rugged and wild' to encourage invertebrates.'

A large dragonfly welcomes Cook and Pietersen back to the pavilion in Bangladesh in 2011.

11

'SOME WIDER FIELD':
The Cricket Naturalist in Literature

A few years ago a friend asked me what my favourite natural history book was.

'*Waterlog*', I said, after not many moments' thought.

'But that's a swimming book!' she protested.

True. It's an account of how Roger Deakin swam (the whole wild swimming movement really derives from his minor masterpiece) his way around Britain, via rivers, lakes, tarns and estuaries.

Except it is the most superb piece of sustained writing about the natural world: a kind of otter's-eye view of the universe.

So OK: a swimming book doesn't count – what else?

The Complete Memoirs of George Sherston by Siegfried Sassoon.

The Country Child by Alison Uttley.

The Shining Levels by John Wyatt.

But all these are books about people too: a fictionalised three-volume autobiography that ranges through fox-hunting and trench warfare on the Western Front to later First World War postings to the Middle East; a children's novel about a girl growing up on a farm; the memoir of a National Park ranger in the Lake District.

The point is, however, that in all these books the natural world is perpetually present and described with exquisite sensitivity. I'd go so far as to say that I don't think of Siegfried Sassoon as primarily a war poet but as one of our finest nature writers.

Much current Nature Writing, on the other hand, I don't warm to. Its resurgence in recent years is largely – as with so many publishing bandwagons – down to one book: Helen Macdonald's *H is for Hawk*, after a precedent established by another pensive and distinguished memoir, Richard Mabey's *Nature Cure*. As happened after the success of *Fever Pitch* and *Bridget Jones's Diary*, however, other publishers' determination to grab some market share of this lucrative genre has seen it gain its own section in the bookshop, and become predictably over-published and … generic. The stereotypical volume about How I Spent Time With beavers/hares/waterfalls/granite and found myself/

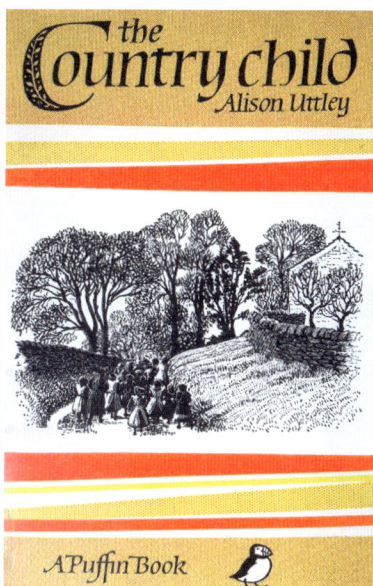

cured my anxiety/stopped over-eating, or the books by people who make themselves go and dwell in a dark shack in a forest for a year, or set out to live like a pine marten, or follow the migration route to Mauretania to find out how it feels to be a cuckoo: such books (I stopped after one or two) seems either a stunt, along the lines of the travel writing boom of recent years that led people to haul fridges round Ireland, or to belong in the Mind, Body and Spirit section.

It's also *not funny*. The natural world isn't comic or tragic (whatever the anthropomorphic melodramas increasingly imposed on wildlife documentaries as a little baby turtle takes its first frail steps towards the sea while the marauding gulls circle . . .). It just is, which seems to encourage so many contemporary nature writers to be so *earnest* about it.

'Nothing was more human than direct speech', observes Paul Theroux's narrator in his novel *My Secret History*. I like books that make me laugh, and it is people – us – that are funny. It's one of the best things writing can do, and it doesn't happen often enough. And of all the sporting literatures, cricket's is the funniest – by a mile. 'A sense of humour is a sense of proportion,' as someone said: not everything is serious, and actually the more certain things really are serious, even critical, perhaps tragic, the more important and corrective become the things that are not serious. But to write about the natural world and allow space for a sense of humour you also have to write about people being people. You cannot just write about nature.

In any case, there is not that much you can say about a hare. It can't talk, it can't hold a conversation, and we haven't a clue what it's thinking or feeling, if anything at all. It can't be funny: it isn't pretending to anything – it just is. A nature-writing 'classic' like J. A. Baker's *The Peregrine* is unreadable: it's just someone looking up into the sky and cataloguing birds flying, day after day. And when the human involvement is reduced to a first-person author bearing witness, or gazing in mute worship at some epiphanic sighting, the most we can hope for is usually a vague transcendentalism or religiosity. It's also fundamentally introspective: it may mean something to them; it can't so much to the rest of us. Above all, so much of modern nature writing seems predicated on the natural world being some discrete Narnia to be accessed through the wardrobe only by leaving our Normal World behind.

But our entire apprehension and appreciation of the world around us is mediated by, in fact created by, us, as active human beings. We do everything we do within it; whatever we do brings us into contact with it, if we did but notice, from the trees in our street on the way to work to the starlings snapping up crumbs from our lunchtime sandwich in the park to the holes munched in our row of lettuces to our boots clagged with mud because rain, clay soil and innumerable feet on the daily dog-walk have combined to pulverise the grass on the common into quagmire. It's part of *everything* else we do.

'Cricket', writes C.L.R. James in *Beyond a Boundary* (we have finally got to it), 'is first and foremost a dramatic spectacle. It belongs with the theatre, ballet, opera and dance.' Quite. And so should be nature writing. And cricket writing. And they needn't – shouldn't – be separate, let alone mutually exclusive.

It is certainly more difficult these days to write about cricket *and* the natural world. County and Test grounds are being constructed from scratch as concrete bowls, rather than having evolved from open fields. When I used to watch the John Player League on the BBC on Sunday afternoons from the late Sixties John Arlott *could* see gulls and crows – because games would frequently be televised from bucolic grounds like Tring and Moreton-in-Marsh. At first-class level the game has become unrelievedly commercial, even industrialised: the players are actually auctioned off. Winning is a business. Distraction is the enemy of focus, of *building pressure*. In *Britain's Lost Cricket Festivals* Chris Arnot asked Surrey's chief executive if the players these days enjoyed county games being taken out to the kind of sylvan grounds I like watching cricket at - the 'festival' grounds.

'Do you want an honest answer?'

'Yes.'

'No.'

So for the most part we have to go back to a time before this separation occurred: the Edwardian era. In a sense the nineteenth century was finally brought to an end by the First World War; that's when the world entered the modern age: machine guns, mustard gas, tanks and aerial bombardment gave it no choice. But during these charmed early years of the century life in rural England, certainly, carried on as it had always done, which is why, for young men who had eagerly volunteered to sign up and found themselves cowering in trenches, the only poetic means they had to express themselves with was pastoral. Which is why they had eyes for the poppies and ears for the birdsong even as the trees were being blasted to stumps.

And pastoral was what the game of cricket still was then. Here is

Hugh De Selincourt in *The Cricket Match*, enumerating the 'thousand other awarenesses' that touch his protagonist Paul Gauvinier amid 'the sunshine and a good game of cricket': 'little vibrations from the children and spectators; the line of the hills; the softness of the grass; the feel of his flannels; the throbbing longing to make some runs; … the soaring swallows…' 'Awareness' is the key word – substitute 'mindfulness' in current parlance - and scoring runs is only one of a thousand such!

And here is Donald Cameron in A. G. Macdonell's comic classic *England, Their England*, springing out of the charabanc that has

In 1990 Gloucestershire were still taking games out to picturesque Moreton-in-Marsh in the Cotswolds. Note Jack Russell in trademark floppy hat.

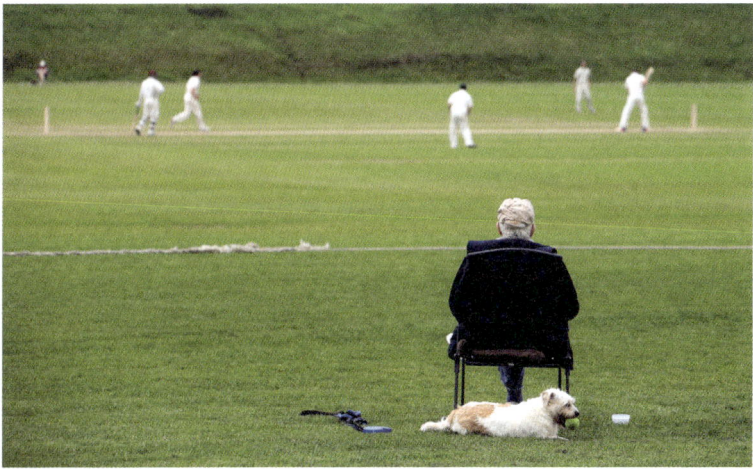

brought him down with the gentlemen from London for their match in the Kent village of Fordenden, 'enchanted by his first sight of rural England ... the real England, unspoilt by factories and financiers and tourists and hustle':

> Bees lazily drifted. White butterflies flapped their aimless way among the gardens. Delphiniums, larkspur, tiger-lilies, evening-primrose, monk's-hood, sweet-peas, swaggered brilliantly above the box hedges, the wooden palings, and the rickety gates.

But though Macdonell's principal task is to modulate the hilarious farce of his cricket match, at every turn the natural world plays a part. The slow bowling of the home side's rate-collector is cunningly delivered 'at the extreme edge of the crease so as to secure a background of dark laurels instead of a dazzling white screen'; the apoplectic

The 'thousand other awarenesses' of a game of cricket: Sheffield Collegiate CC.

fast-bowling blacksmith, having tightened his belt yet another notch and shaken out yet another inch in his braces, has 'marched off like a Pomeranian grenadier and vanished over the brow of the hill':

> At last, after a long stillness, the ground shook, the grasses waved violently, small birds arose with shrill clamours, a loud puffing alarmed the butterflies, and the blacksmith, looking more like Venus Anadyomene than ever, came thundering over the crest.

With scores level and last men in, the blacksmith hits his first ball

> up in the air at an enormous height. It went up and up, until it became difficult to focus it properly against the deep, cloudless blue of the sky, and it carried with it the hopes and fears of an English village. Up and up it went and then at the top it seemed to hang motionless in the air, poised like a hawk...

The natural world, you see, has a metaphoric presence too in the cricket literature of this time: the factories and the financiers and tourists and hustle had not yet crowded it out to the extent that you had to make a point of looking for it, and this was the imagery that came readily to hand. Early in *Cricket Country* Edmund Blunden looks back on the village cricket in the Kent of his childhood, and thinks of 'those games, coming and going like wild flowers'.

Cricket writers were still able to write in this way when Alan Ross went to the Caribbean in 1960. Those white pigeons which flew up and away from the ground at Port of Spain after the Second Test disfigured by rioting and 'took the late sun on their wings as they dipped against the hills': are they a felicitous metaphor of the spirit of cricket itself temporarily taking flight?

Back then Ross could quite unselfconsciously write a travel book about a cricket tour: from the Scorebook at the end of *Through the Caribbean* it doesn't appear the MCC party played a game on Tobago, but Ross goes there anyway, and assumes you're happy to read a whole paragraph exclusively about the bird life.

> Living in Tobago it would be impossible not to become a
> naturalist. Flowers, fish, shell, birds, animals: in what would
> one specialise?
>   . . . the birds are as sociable as they are voluble. The
> hooting mot-mot, with pendulum flight, and tail as long
> as its tailored, green-gold body and reddish waistcoat,
> haunts our windows in the search for food. The jacamar, a
> smaller-six-inch version of the mot-mot, makes a noise
> like a referee's whistle. Walking through the estate here, you
> can hear and see mocking-birds and keskedees, tanagers
> and emerald humming-birds, grackles and golden-eyed
> thrushes. Farther north, cocoa-birds and parrots, spinetails
> and trogons fly in and out of the woods with the twittering
> restlessness of women at a cocktail party.

(I guess people don't write metaphors like the last one nowadays either.)

But tours back then lasted for months and took in many provincial sides in far-flung outposts: MCC went out before Christmas and were still playing British Guiana in March. Neville Cardus wrote an entire chapter of his book on the 1936–7 Ashes series about the voyage out to Australia. Today's international cricketers fly in to a country and go straight into back-to-back Tests (which may go towards explaining why in 2021 England were so discombobulated, even outraged, by the turning pitch they encountered at Ahmedabad.) The whole world is an endless tour; it is the schedule of rock bands, not cricket travellers.

CRICKET COUNTRY
EDMUND BLUNDEN

Introduction by Benny Green

THE PAVILION LIBRARY

THROUGH THE
CARIBBEAN
ENGLAND IN THE WEST INDIES, 1960

ALAN ROSS

THE PAVILION LIBRARY

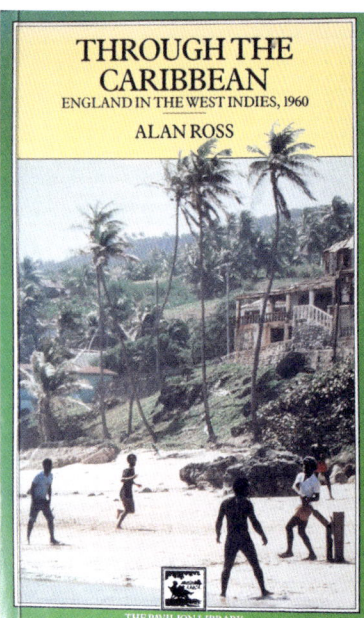

This also means that today's international cricketers don't have much time to develop a hinterland or explore a country: as soon as the Test finishes they're on a plane to the next continent for the next Big Bash.

I'm in interested in that word 'naturalist', though. Today's terminology either denotes a leisure activity (*birdwatcher*) or a more specifically scientific vocation: *ecologist, botanist, lepidopterist* – and you're encouraged to specialise. But a naturalist – I wonder if Sir David Attenborough is the last of the line – is something in between. It's not quite a professional occupation, but neither is it just about taking pleasure in the natural world. It speaks of someone who is interested in – even a proselytiser for – the natural: in how things are if you just leave them be (and not just the natural world).

Either way, that natural world is not held at arm's length, as an elsewhere to be travelled to. 'Witnessing these things', writes Edmund Blunden in *Cricket Country*, watching two crows on a hill cleverly vanish down an old rabbit burrow to evade a bounding dog, 'we wondered much for all our love of human beings and their sports and games if there could be anything better than wandering as Richard Jefferies did, and the joys of the naturalist became singularly attractive.'

Cricket Country, also Edwardian in its milieu (though not published until 1944) and written, like Sassoon's, in the shadow of the Western Front, Blunden having set down his experiences in another classic First World War memoir, *Undertones of War*, is a kind of manifesto for the cricket naturalist. 'Digressions may multiply in these pages,' he says, encouragingly, almost at the start, and his recollections of the rustic, occasionally shambolic local cricket matches of his childhood have an oddly dreamlike quality, at once opaque and hallucinatory. But in Chapter 3, reflecting on a particular game that had taken an age to get going while all its rustic participants made their unhurried way to the field, Blunden writes:

> The game gave me some sense of being rather a continuation of rural labours than a sport and a pastime. It was carried through as earnestly as, say, measuring the hops in a bin, or bringing a team of horses over the bridge with that queer thing a car steering along from the opposite direction; where there was skill, it was applied with the same attentiveness as the skill of grafting a tree.

You couldn't take cricket out of the natural world, in other words: it belonged in, was part of, the country. As Blunden himself puts it very near the end of the book,

> I can ever feel that the game which made me write at all is not terminated at the boundary, but is reflected beyond, is echoed and varied out there among the gardens and the barns, the dells and the thickets, and belongs to some wider field.

Acknowledgements and Bibliography:

Thank you to all the following for their help with the research and pictures: Clare Adams, Heather Lomas and Robert Curphey at the MCC, Mark Ashdown of the Bristol Tree Forum, Simon Barnes, Caroline Buckland, Bob and Jane Carr at the Quince Tree Press (for the extracts from *Carr's Dictionary of Extra-Ordinary Cricketers*), Blaise Drummond, Tessa Boase, Jonathan Campion, Hector Capelletti at the Yahooovercowcorner blog, Stephen Chalke of Fairfield Books and John Barclay (for the extract from *The Appeal of the Championship*), Will Ellsworth-Jones, Mark Elson at the *Forest Review*, John Fletcher, Lady Antonia Fraser (verse from 'Harold and Cricket' © Lady Antonia Fraser 2020), Mathew Frith, Tim Gardiner, Caroline Gascoigne, Peter Gillman, Mike Hall of the North West Fungus Group, Richard Humphrey, David Lancaster, Alan Leitch of Compass (for the inspired title), Stephen Lovell, Paula McHugh of Belfast Health and Social Care Trust, Dave Merrell at Cinderford Cricket Club, Graham Morris of Cricketpix, Doug Morton, Stephen Moss, Matthew Oates, Gareth Parry of Gloucestershire Wildlife Trust, Steve Proctor, Philip Sinclair at Kirkby Lonsdale Cricket Club, Stuart Tree, Peter Watson, Rod Webb and Hugh Sullivan of *Hastings Independent Press*, David Welch, Paul Wood, and everyone who responded to the Twitter appeals.

The following works were helpful, and are recommended:

Chris Arnot, *Britain's Lost Cricket Grounds* (Aurum, 2011) and *Britain's Lost Cricket Festivals* (Aurum, 2013)

John Barclay, *The Appeal of the Championship* (Fairfield Books, 2002)

Edmund Blunden, *Cricket Country* (Pavilion, 1985)

Neville Cardus, *A Field of Tents and Waving Colours* (Safe Haven, 2018)

J. L. Carr, *Carr's Dictionary of Extra-Ordinary Cricketers* (Aurum/Quince Tree Press, 2005)

Roger Deakin, *Waterlog* (Vintage, 2000)

Hugh de Selincourt, *The Cricket Match* (OUP, 1979)

Ramachandra Guha, *A Corner of a Foreign Field* (Picador, 2003)

C. L. R. James, *Beyond a Boundary* (Yellow Jersey, 2005)

Brian Levison, *Remarkable Village Cricket Grounds* (Pavilion, 2018)

A. G. Macdonell, *England, Their England* (Picador, 1983)

Michael Meyer (ed.), *Summer Days: Writers on Cricket* (OUP, 1981)

Derek Moore, *Birds: Coping with an Obsession* (New Holland, 2013)

Alan Ross, *Through the Caribbean* (Pavilion, 1986)

Siegfried Sassoon, *The Complete Memoirs of George Sherston* (Faber, 1972)

Martin Smith, *Not in My Day, Sir: Cricket Letters to the Daily Telegraph* (Aurum, 2011)

Alison Uttley, *The Country Child* (Puffin, 1966)

John Wyatt, *The Shining Levels* (Penguin, 1976)

Andy Bull, 'Badgers, crows and the war on cricket pitches', The Spin, *Guardian*, 23 April 2013.

Simon Burnton, 'Cricket's storied siblings, from missionaries to the seven Fosters', The Spin, *Guardian*, 30 March 2021.

Tim Gardiner, 'More runs, fewer crickets!', *Bulletin of the Amateur Entomologists' Society*, January 2010, https://researchgate. net/publication/333699949_More_runs_ fewer_crickets.

Abhishek Mukherjee, '30 instances of cricket's bitter-sweet affair with animals', www.cricketcountry.com, 5 October 2016.

Arunabha Sengupta, 'The day India ended England's home rule', www.cricketcountry.com, 20 September 2016.

Rob Smyth, 'The scariest Test England ever played: terror at the hands of the West Indies', *Guardian*, 13 August 2017.

Mike Williamson, 'The fungus that floored the Aussies', www.espncricinfo.com, 25 July 2015.

Picture Credits:

Graham Morris, Cricketpix: 2, 12–13, 16, 19, 29 (bottom), 37, 47, 62–3, 64, 65, 86, 96, 105, 107 (left), 108 (right), 111 (top), 112, 126, 127, 128, 134–5

David Darrell-Lambert, www.birdbrainuk. com: 10, 108 (left), 116

Getty Images: 11, 29, 40 (both Patrick Eagar), 99, 102

Alan Duncan Photography, Folkestone: 15

Mary Evans Picture Library: 17, 107 (right)

MCC: 23, 51 (top) (Clare Adams), 109,

Tim Gardiner: 24, 49, 121 (top left and right, bottom left)

Historic Environment Scotland (Britain from Above): 27

Alamy: 29 (bottom), 35 (top right), 50, 61 (bottom), 111 (bottom)

Graham Coster: 30, 32, 33, 35 (top left), 43, 70 (top, bottom right), 74, 75, 79, 87

Stuart Tree, www.stuarttreesports.co.uk: 35 (bottom), 97 (top)

Doug Morton: 36 (top)

Bristol Tree Forum: 38 (top)

Richard Humphrey, Geograph: 38 (bottom)

Gareth Parry, Gloucestershire Wildlife Trust: 48

Ashley Western: 51 (bottom)

Philip Sinclair: 55

PA Photos: 57

Glamorgan CCC: 61 (top)

Jonathan Campion: 66

John Fletcher, https:// highburycricketclub.fletch-design. co.uk/: 69 (top)

Darran Lambert: 69 (bottom)

Doug Mounsey: 70 (bottom left)

Peter Gillman: 73

Paul Wood, thestreettree.com: 77, 78

© Belfast Health & Social Care Trust: 83 (left)

Wakefield Permanent Art Collection (purchased 1945); photo: Jerry Hardman-Jones): 83 (right)

© Royal Air Force Museum 2021: 84

Private Collection© David Inshaw/ Bridgeman Images: 85

Sussex Cricket Museum: 91

The Forest Review: 94 (left)

Geoff Robinson Photography: 94 (right)

Hector Capelletti: 97 (bottom)

Stephen Lovell: 100

Steve Proctor: 115

Matthew Oates: 119

Neil Phillips: 121 (bottom right)

Punch Cartoon Library/Topfoto: 124

Index